HEART OPEN, BODY AWAKE

Heart
Open

FOUR STEPS TO
EMBODIED SPIRITUALITY

Body
Awake

Susan Aposhyan

SHAMBHALA

Shambhala Publications
2129 13th Street
Boulder, Colorado 80302
www.shambhala.com

Cover art: Brosko/iStock
Cover design: Michel Vrana
Interior design: Gopa & Ted2, Inc.

9 8 7 6 5 4 3 2 1

First Edition
Printed in the United States of America

♾ This edition is printed on acid-free paper that meets the
American National Standards Institute z39.48 Standard.
♻ This book is printed on 30% postconsumer recycled paper.
For more information please visit www.shambhala.com.
Shambhala Publications is distributed worldwide by
Penguin Random House, Inc., and its subsidiaries.

Library of Congress Cataloging-in-Publication Data
Names: Aposhyan, Susan M., author.
Title: Heart open, body awake: four steps to embodied spirituality /
Susan Aposhyan.
Description: Boulder, Colorado: Shambhala, [2021] | Includes
bibliographical references.
Identifiers: LCCN 2020043663 | ISBN 9781611809404 (trade paperback)
Subjects: LCSH: Human body—Religious aspects. | Spirituality.
Classification: LCC BL604.B64 A66 2021 | DDC 204—dc23
LC record available at https://lccn.loc.gov/2020043663

To my mother, from whom I learned so deeply
about joy and suffering.

Contents

Introduction

M Y FIRST MEMORY of the embodied spirituality that underlies all my work began with stars. When I was a child, the dark infinity of the sky was overflowing with them. It seemed that the universe was composed almost entirely of twinkling celestial bodies. There was also my small child's body, huddled in an old wool blanket and feeling blissfully overwhelmed by the vastness of it all. More specifically, the seeing and feeling of the stars and the vastness felt somehow continuous, as if without any separation between the little "me-ness" that was watching and the titanic size and beauty of that which I saw. My body was small, but the feelings it was hosting were as large as that sky.

Growing up in the sixties in Virginia, experiences like this were plentiful. The world was quiet enough and dark enough. Nature was strong enough to dominate my child's mind. Lying in the grasses, watching the endless circuits of the clouds. Hearing the insects conducting their business in meadows. Running through the forest that was itself an endless dance of light and leaves, filled with the symphony of many birdcalls. And then there was the water—rain, creeks, rivers, and waves—flowing over rocks, moving, always moving. Enchanting, beguiling, intoxicating, engulfing, bathing the eyes and the ears and thereby washing through the interior of my body. Nothing was left untouched by these experiences. In having them, I was also sampling the way in which feeling and seeing and hearing and smelling and even tasting—honeysuckle, blackberries, rose hips—could take place under the aegis of a larger continuity. There was no barrier between my body and nature. I was directly absorbed into the natural world, educated by it, without a thought of separation or distinction.

In contrast, the human world seemed quite odd and disjointed, and its denizens—the people around me—hollow, unnaturally subdued, as if they were merely playing at being alive rather than actually living. As I grew older, I saw that they were making deliberate choices to ignore life, to wall themselves off from it, electing instead to live within very small parameters, and deceiving themselves and others in the process. I soon learned about the pain that came with this artificial separation of one individual self from the continuity of life. As I became intimate with the pain of my family and friends, I always saw the solution to that pain as reestablishing continuity with nature.

The perceptions I'm remembering and describing are quite visual in my mind. When I looked at nature, it seemed everywhere to belong to an effortless universal continuum. But when I looked at people, they appeared to be somehow cut off from this continuum, standing outside it like cartoon figures cut out of a drawing. Eventually I learned that this strange disconnect between people and their natural surroundings was part of a larger existential confusion in our culture. I became interested in psychology and in the possibility it offered to understand this confusion and, as a result, to help relieve human suffering.

Religion was apparently another system that was supposed to resolve the pain. I faithfully went to church as a young girl, and I watched and listened. But I simply didn't see the continuity of healing that I beheld in nature. I didn't see the cartoon figures becoming reconnected to the universe. In my church, I really didn't see much happening at all.

Finally, on the Easter Sunday of my thirteenth year, I resolved to leave the Christian church. Watching the congregation with the exquisitely intense eye of adolescent arrogance, I determined that no one in the room, including the minister, was touched by the words or the music or the presence of other people, let alone a feeling of God. Not a single person there seemed to be in touch with the vital force of their own heart.

Less than a decade later, after time spent meditating, teaching dance, studying psychology, and practicing counseling, I would discover Body-Mind Centering®, the lifework of Bonnie Bainbridge Cohen. In her beautiful body of material, I found the inspiration that allowed the disparate threads of my various interests to begin slowly to weave together.

I have spent my life studying what it means to be human in all its aspects. I have studied the body, the mind, psychology, various religions, spirituality, art, anatomy, physiology, neuroscience, evolution, movement, birth, and death. I have worked with thousands of people, individually and in groups, in classes and retreats; as a psychotherapist, a bodyworker, a movement teacher, and a meditation teacher. And from all this, there is one thing I know for sure: *we are all in this together.*

One of the basic tenets of embodied spirituality is that we each have to begin where we are, as we are, with whatever is arising in this body right now. On one level, our individuality is a crazy swirl of thoughts, emotions, sensations, and beliefs happening in our bodies moment to moment. With awareness, we can emerge from this swirl into an open clarity, resonant with the world around us. From here, we can begin to work together to wake up humanity and avert the planetary crisis that may end us. Even though we are all coming from different places, different views, we are truly all in this together.

I first began teaching about embodiment in the 1980s. At that time, the use of the term was rare. Now it is ubiquitous. Yet when people refer to the word *embodiment*, they are usually approaching the body in some cognitively dominant manner. They remain in the realm of ideas, thinking about the body and telling it what to do. All too often this realm of ideas is mixed up with mainstream cultural tropes about how the body should look, feel, and be. I want to reclaim the word for its deeper, wilder purpose.

Embodiment is something that all the other creatures on the planet exhibit and something we adult humans have systematically attempted to snuff out in ourselves. We can define embodiment as the continuous, complete, and free flow of cognition, emotion, and behavior through our bodies. Practically speaking, this means that whatever is occurring within our beings is allowed to organically express itself in our behavior. Is this dangerous stuff that leads to chaos? Not really. Through the course of this book, as we explore the physiological, evolutionary, and neurological bases of human embodiment, we will come to understand that our drive to live harmoniously with others is deeply embedded in us. Thus, as we practice embodiment, we tend to become more compassionate toward, more connected to, and more considerate of the world around us.

This mutual unfolding of inward awareness and outward expression is key to understanding the connection between embodiment and spirituality. Embodied spirituality is an approach to life that says the more familiar we become with the various aspects and layers of our lives as bodily beings, the more connected and engaged we will be with others and with the whole world of our inner and outer experience. Perhaps not everyone would call this spirituality—and I would certainly never insist anyone do so. But my experience, and that of many others, is that the depth, intensity, and sense of wonder that results from practicing this way of being truly are best described with terms like *spirit* and *sacred*.

Embodied spirituality is an emergent discipline. As the dominance of organized religion wanes, more of us are allowing our own spiritualities to unfold from within rather than following the strictures of the patriarchal religions with which most of us grew up. This reverses a deep historical move in Western civilization wherein, as Europe transitioned from pagan traditions to Christianity, people turned away from the body and female-centered spirituality. Thus, it is not coincidental that as our cultural exploration of spirituality becomes more personal, it is simultaneously becoming more inclusive of the body.

Many approaches to psychology, spirituality, and bodywork are interested in embodiment. In order to take these approaches beyond the cognitive, we have to begin with our bodies in very direct ways. We have to spend time expanding our attention to include sensation, the language of the body. We have to learn the delicate art of allowing the body to move its physiology back to a healthy freedom. Finally, we actually need to excavate, realize, express, and clear out all the old, accumulated patterns that we have engrained in our bodies. These patterns that kept us alive and safe when they emerged often remain long after their usefulness has ended.

I have seen embodiment practices help people heal their physical ailments; resolve old, deeply embedded emotional patterns; liberate themselves from the tyranny of trauma; and go much further with manifesting kindness and leadership. And I have experienced all this myself. I have become a humbler, friendlier, more optimistic person. Of course, there are no guarantees, and there will be bumps along the way, but if approached openly and maturely, deepening into embodiment seems to offer nearly infinite returns.

Embodied spirituality is emerging in myriad ways: mindfulness, meditation, centering prayer, yoga, Sufism, eco-dharma, and heart-centered practices. It can be fruitfully practiced in these and many other ways, and the teachings and practices in this book can be used to support whatever spiritual practices you already have. *Heart Open, Body Awake* presents a very body-centered approach to embodied spirituality, articulated in four steps. These steps are found throughout many approaches to spirituality. The way that we bring them together here allows one to develop from the inside out in a uniquely embodied way. Without further ado, the four steps are:

1. Open your heart.
2. Feel your body.
3. Allow what you discover in your heart and body to move you.
4. Discover the continuity between your heart, your body, and the world in its immediacy.

We can name them even more simply: open, feel, allow, connect. I love this simplicity—and yet, as you have likely experienced, this is complex terrain.

As the pinwheel in the figure opposite suggests, these steps are not meant to be understood merely in a linear way. Indeed, although I list them as concrete steps and refer to them that way throughout the book, the "steps" are actually both actions and states of being, with all the complexity, ambiguity, and nuance

that lived states of being inevitably entail. For this reason, you will find that the four steps, though loosely aligned with the four parts of this book, all intertwine with each other. They are sequential in one sense but more deeply are the warp and weft of the whole book, which is focused on helping you slowly unpack each of these states of being through stories, practices, and theoretical explanations. Though the four steps sound simple, they are running against the habits of our egoic selves. If we want to develop a truly embodied approach to spirituality, we have to practice each of these states of being in their myriad facets.

Part One of this book, "Heart of Humanity," introduces the magic of the human heart, some of its physiology, and some practices to begin exploring it. Obviously, this section is most explicitly focused on opening the heart, but the other three steps of feeling, allowing, and connecting are intrinsically involved.

Part Two, "Body of Life," initiates our discussion of feeling, the second step, and also introduces the third step—allowing our authentic expression through movement, sensation, and physiology. Further attention is given to allowing our bodily experience permission to express itself and to how this process of feeling and allowing begins to dissolve the walls of our individual encapsulation and result in a sense of oneness with the world. I often refer to that oneness as "the unitive state"—the reality that each of our hearts really is the center of the universe.

Part Three, "Deepening and Blossoming," fleshes out further details of feeling your body—a tour of the inner anatomical world and some of its access points. Part Three introduces Embodiment Practice as a formal practice approach that I have developed over the last four decades. While there are many embodiment practices, the Embodiment Practice presented here is intended to be an all-inclusive tool to reintegrate the adult human body and mind. Not only does Embodiment Practice include feeling all the parts of your body as they present themselves to you, it is also the best method I know for exploring the third step of embodied spirituality: allowing the sensations you feel to move through your being in their own unique way. I share more details and specifics regarding Embodiment Practice here than I have done before in written form. This begins with my definition of embodiment, given as an antidote to the oversimplification of its current use in popular culture, and continues through a step-by-step introduction to Embodiment Practice so you can begin to practice it on your own. I hope the numerous guided practices in Part Three will help you experience how step two (feeling) evolves into step three (allowing), which opens onto step four (connecting).

Part Four, "The Path of Opening and Connecting," completes the cycle by looking at how the fruition of connecting, the fourth and final step, manifests. There are chapters on spiritual fruition, applying embodiment in death and dying, and a chapter to support you in using embodiment and the four steps in your personal spiritual development.

Over the last twenty years of study and practice, I published two books that dealt with body-mind integration and its applications in psychotherapy. After finishing my second book, I felt ready to write about how spirituality was a hidden key to understanding the paradox of our humanity, which somehow spans the animal and the divine. I dreamed of a book that would reveal the profundity of our human drive to unite those polarities—body and mind, creaturely and spiritual. Necessarily, it would open and close with a study of what I've come to believe is the essential link between body and spirit: the human heart. It is this book that you hold in your hands.

PART ONE
Heart of Humanity

1

DISCOVERING THE HEART

The way is not in the sky. The way is in the heart.

—SHAKYAMUNI BUDDHA

I ONCE DISSECTED the body of a very interesting man. One of his ears appeared to have been bitten off by human teeth. The ear was sewn back on but sloppily, slightly off its original spot. He had some tattoos that seemed to offer clues about his life. I can't recall the specifics, but I remember my fantasized images: waterside bars and dockworkers. And he was exceptionally strong in one of his psoas muscles, the deepest of the hip flexors—a heavy equipment operator? But his heart held the most striking anomaly of all. He had a hard calcification, a little smaller than half a baseball, on the side of his heart. I was amazed that someone could live with such a growth. There was no evidence that this had killed him. He had lived, literally, with a hardened heart.

There seem to be so many reasons and ways in which we harden or close our hearts. We shut down. We inure ourselves to loss and fear. We prioritize safety and comfort over our emotional realities. Many of us are afraid to feel sensation in our hearts. When we feel such sensation, we wonder, "Is that a heart attack? Is there something physically wrong with my heart?" Consciously feeling our physical hearts can be a step toward courageous awareness. When people are suffering from a terrible heartbreak or loss, their hearts often ache. I wonder if this ache is the sensation of the heart tissue, which is muscular, cramping dramatically as it opens to its new life.

I heard a story about a girl preparing for her bat mitzvah. During her study, her rabbi kept telling the class that they were placing the teachings on their hearts. Finally, this girl shot up her hand and asked the rabbi, "Why are we placing the teachings on our hearts? Why don't we just put the teachings into our hearts?" The rabbi responded, "Oh, well, that's because neither you nor I have the power to place the teachings in our hearts, but if we place them on our hearts then when our hearts break, the teachings will fall in."

We're all familiar with the phrase "open your heart," but what does that really mean? In order to understand opening our hearts experientially and to take it on as a practice, we first need to establish a sense of basic familiarity. We need to discover our hearts.

Our hearts are constantly opening and closing. This happens on many levels. On the most obvious level, the chambers of our hearts open and close with every heartbeat as they take in our blood and then send it on. Our hearts are primarily composed of cardiac muscle, and like all muscle, the heart's fibers shorten and lengthen. The muscle composing each chamber of the heart shortens and lengthens with each beat. Beyond this, some of the cardiac muscle fibers can be shortened ongoingly. This is one way that our hearts can be relatively closed. When our hearts break emotionally, this muscle fiber that has been chronically shortened can lengthen and join back in with the pulsation of the heart. Our hearts can break open physically and emotionally. They can shine forth. The fibers that were habitually shortened can lengthen, even after decades.

Cardiac muscle shortens and lengthens in the same way skeletal muscle does, through filaments sliding together and apart. Hold your hands out in front of you and let your fingers slide together and apart. When a group of skeletal muscle fibers stays shortened, we call it a spasm or a cramp. If we gently move the cramping area, eventually it joins back into the symphony of shortening and lengthening muscle. In our hearts, the muscle movement is involuntary, responding to a complex of neurological and chemical inputs. When we want to shorten or lengthen skeletal muscle, it suffices to merely have the intention. I see my glass of water. I want to pick it up. All of the muscles in my arm respond accordingly.

With cardiac muscle, the input is less direct, more complex. We might think, "I want to open my heart." For some of us, nothing might happen at first. For others, our hearts might magically respond. Over time, all of us can slowly weave together a series of neural networks that will allow the cardiac muscle to respond to our intention.

Another way we open and close our hearts is by dilating and constricting the blood vessels that circulate within and around the heart. Our heart cells produce a hormone called atrial natriuretic peptide (ANP), which is involved in the constriction and dilation of our blood vessels. I wonder whether, when we feel a sudden flush of heart opening, this happens through a release of ANP. Sadly, this is not a question that has been explored scientifically, so it remains speculative. Whatever the case, opening our hearts feels good, and with it comes a greater ability to connect with others.

When our hearts break emotionally, we can understand it in

a way that makes us smaller: "I am bad. The world is bad. Love is always painful. I'll never love again." When we respond this way, then our hearts close more.

Awakening the heart seems essential to all spiritual disciplines. We bring our hands together in front of our hearts to pray. In interfaith dialogues, I have witnessed extreme fundamentalists agreeing that we each have to discover for ourselves what it is that touches our hearts.

On a physical level, the heart is an amazing organ. It has the strongest electromagnetic field of any organ within the body. The heart's electrical field is between fifty and sixty times stronger than that of the brain, which is the second strongest field generator in the human body. The heart's electromagnetic field is *five thousand* times stronger than that of the brain. This field radiates out from the heart in a torus shape, including the whole body and much of the space around it.

William Harvey, the English physician who first delineated the physiological role of the heart in his 1628 book, *On the*

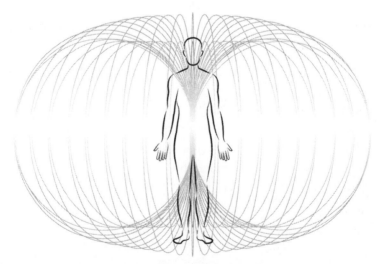

Electromagnetic field of the heart

Motion of the Heart and Blood in Animals, likened the heart to the king or the sun of the body. Modern culture has shifted that place of honor from the heart to the brain. We have placed reason and intellect above the heart. Neuropsychologist and author Paul Pearsall sees this as a fundamental confusion, similar to early cultural beliefs that the sun orbits around the earth. Our cultural fixation on the brain is one reason why so many of us need to discover or rediscover our hearts—a basic sense of familiarity has been lost. But that doesn't mean that the brain is irrelevant, any more than the earth became irrelevant once we learned that it actually orbits the sun and not vice versa. The brain and the heart are intricately connected.

THE DANCE BETWEEN THE BRAIN AND THE HEART

Which of these organs is more powerful? The answers are less clear-cut than they might first appear. The brain gathers information from a wide swath of internal and external sensory data, but it bases its decisions on habit and repetition. This is fundamental to the brain's physiology.

"Neurons that fire together wire together"—this is the original and still fundamental description of brain functioning posited by Donald Hebb in 1949. This principle is so central to neuropsychology that we call it Hebbian theory. In other words, the nervous system is strongly based on conditioning. Repeating a behavior is much easier than changing a behavior because of this tendency.

Furthermore, the nervous system doesn't have its own sensory nerve endings. It can't feel itself and therefore doesn't recognize whether its decisions *feel* harmonious or not. Finally, once we give our rational selves the ultimate power over our decisions, we tend to ignore any information that counters rationality. The rational brain is not good at listening to the heart or any other part of us when it is used to having unilateral power. We all know the feeling of the brain obsessively telling us what needs to be done right now—never backing off and not easily compromising until we have satisfied its demands.

In contrast, the heart is very spacious and relaxed with its sense of direction. If we ignore what feels right in our hearts, they will not jump up and down to get our attention. In fact, it can take us years to circle back around and remember that making a particular choice never really felt completely right. The ideal situation seems to be one in which the brain takes the role of advising the heart. With the brain as the consultant and the heart as the final arbiter, we arrive at decisions that both make sense and feel right.

The HeartMath Institute, a consulting and research group out of Boulder Creek, California, has been studying heart-brain communication for almost three decades.[1] Employing electro-encephalograms, electrocardiograms, and other measurements, researchers have found that when our awareness is centered in our hearts, we are calmer, happier, more resourceful, and more positively connected to others. One of their mottoes is "smart brain, wise heart."

Open Mind

I do not believe in anything, but when I experience something, I know it to be true. —CARL JUNG

When we give our hearts the opportunity to lead, it allows our minds to relax. Thoughts naturally decrease. The same thing occurs with attending to our bodies. Preliminary neuroscientific research indicates that the more awareness one has of sensation, the less one is thinking. In embodied spirituality, we open our hearts and feel the body as a gateway to working with the mind. This eases the inherently delicate and complex task of working with our minds. Since the brain has no sensory nerve endings, we often don't feel when we are treating our mental selves aggressively or even mechanically. We need to lean gently into allowing our minds to open. How did we move away from open-mindedness in the first place? We had it when we were babies.

Babies are such mystics. Before they can talk, before they think in words, they stare at the world with an incredibly open gaze. They see clearly, without labeling or compartmentalizing the world. For them, life is all a miraculous display. That is open-mindedness.

Once we begin talking and thinking in words, the world changes so dramatically and so decisively. That mystical mind becomes lost to most of us. The two-year-old mind of "no" and "mine," "this" and "that," sets in and lays down deep, deep roots.

This developmental change parallels our shift as a species, out of embeddedness in nature and into entanglement in human culture, the shift from animal mysticism to egoic materialism. This is not an argument to go back to nature, to return to our animal natures. It is a call to continue in our personal development toward an embodied humanity, a culture that is able to play with our ability to conceptualize without losing our direct experience.

In these last few thousand years, we have left behind a way of being that was billions of years old. We have moved from being embedded in our world to inhabiting an almost virtual reality, which we are compelled to manipulate. Once we began to label and compartmentalize, the fundamental duality of self and other set in. Either consciously or unconsciously, we are constantly angling toward survival and personal advantage. From this, the pursuit of comfort ensues, and then it is a nearly hopeless mess.

How do we practice opening our minds?

Seeing from the Heart

Pause.

Feel your body. Feel your heart. Rest into your heart and see if it wants to open a bit.

Open your eyes and let them rest on whatever is in front of them. If you can catch it, watch your mind orienting to and labeling what it is seeing. Allow your vision to rest on whatever it is seeing, and give your mind permission to see the colors and light without labeling. Have a sense that you are seeing from your heart.

This practice needs repetition; it evolves over time. It took me a long time to be able to consciously catch the labeling process. As it develops, you can practice hearing from your heart and feeling bodily sensations from your heart. Even tasting and smelling can come from the heart. This helps us bypass the labeling process and open the mind.

Humans are natural storytellers. No matter how open our minds get, our consciousness has a biological tendency to contextualize, to make meaning, to tell ourselves a story about what is happening in our lives and on our paths. Some stories limit us: "This is just the way I am. I can't change it. The world is against me." And some stories open the way to continue our development: "This is what I want. I can feel that I am headed in the right direction. Even though I can't discern the future, I want to keep growing, learning, and healing."

At any given moment, our view of ourselves is either opening the way or obstructing it. Even when we are completely mired in negative emotion or challenge, we can keep opening, telling ourselves, "Right now, I feel overwhelmed, lost, and stuck, but I will get through this, and then I will continue on my path." Treating ourselves kindly during our challenges is an essential aspect of embodied spirituality. It is a practice, and it is one that benefits immeasurably from being centered in the heart. Notice when you are being harsh or critical toward yourself. Change the narrative. Speak kindly. Stay open to what you are learning in each moment.

On a larger level, we can work with being more open with ourselves about who and what we are. What is ego? What is self? What is your true self? What is your conditioned self? At some points along your path, it might benefit you to give yourself permission to just be yourself: "You be you. Live your life." At other points, your heart might open so fully that your awareness of being a particular person becomes inconsequential in the face of being a part of this vast and beautiful universe. Open your heart, open your mind. Let whatever wants to happen, happen.

The Whole Body Is Heart

Most people think of the heart as being on the left side of the chest, but in actuality, the heart fills the whole center of the chest. There is only a bit more on the upper left side. The heart is behind the entire length of the sternum, or breastbone. Take a moment and touch the full length of your sternum firmly from top to bottom, visualizing as you do that your heart is right behind it.

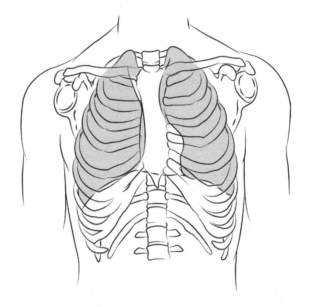

Lung tissue in gray. The white area between the lungs is the small portion of the heart that shows through the lungs' embrace.

Our lungs embrace our hearts, making them truly the wings of the heart. The lungs and heart work so closely together that at times, in a heart transplant, the heart and lungs of the donor are transplanted together into the recipient.

When I first removed and dissected the calcified heart of the tattooed cadaver, I was surprised to see how his lungs remained wrapped around his heart. I imagined that they would flop open, but that was not the case. The organs are far too intrinsically connected for that.

Similarly, the vessels of the circulatory system and the heart work together so inextricably that, in a certain sense, the whole

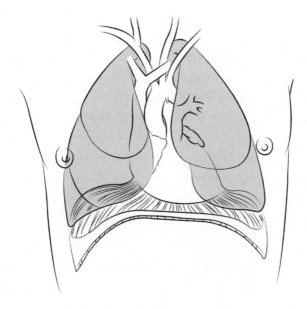

body is heart. Once a very unusual man was telling me about his experiences with "unexpected intimacy." He said that in those moments, he felt "heart all over."

In Chinese medicine, the heart is the center of our beings, governing the rest of the body, all the other major organs and systems. How does it govern? By listening to the blood—its rhythms, its constituents, all the subtle information coming from every cell in the body. The heart guides by resting fully in its place in the center.

In an emotional or energetic sense, the heart is the center of our beings. From the perspective of biomechanics, our center of gravity is lower—the *dan tien*, a Chinese anatomical concept that is essential in martial arts practice. In the most limited definition, the dan tien is the center of gravity, a spot resting a few finger widths below the navel in the center of the pelvis. But in the most expansive meaning, the dan tien includes the entire central channel of the body. A traditional instruction in the practice of tai chi is to rest the "heartmind" in the dan tien. This ensures that we do not disrupt the heart in its resting centrality, nor do we uproot ourselves from the earth. To truly place the heartmind in the dan tien, we must feel our connection to the earth and feel how each part of ourselves rests on the support below it. To fully rest in the support of the earth, each body part, including the feet and the pelvic floor, must yield to gravity. Then all the visceral organs also yield, resting dynamically rather than passively or in a collapsed manner. In this way, the heart is supported by all of the body, especially that which is directly below it.

Secondarily, to rest the heartmind in the dan tien means that we remain centered in our very core rather than getting pulled out of our centers or skewed to the left or the right. As always with the heart, this refers to our literal and physical centers as well as our awareness and presence.

To begin to feel into the heart more fully, let us begin with feeling the beating of our hearts.

Heart Pulsation Meditation

Let yourself sit, lie, or stand in a relaxed and symmetrical position, one in which your whole spine is as long and relaxed as possible.

Get quiet and still enough to feel the beating of your heart. Place your hand on your heart and feel the pulsation with your hand. Even though the heart is in the center of the chest, it is harder to feel the pulsation through the bone. There is a bit more heart protruding to the left of the sternum than to the right. Try placing your hand there. Notice the movement of your chest echoing the beat. If it is difficult to feel your pulse this way, you can put your hand on your carotid artery at the side of your neck or even the radial artery at your wrist. When you are ready, remove your hand and sense the pulsation directly. Spend as long as you like feeling the beat of your heart.

Rest your mind in this sense of pulsation. Relax your body into the rhythm so that your whole body awareness becomes this one pulse.

When you are done, notice how you are feeling and why you stopped when you did. What happened during this heart meditation? Was there a shift in your physical body, in your energetic body? Was there a shift in your state of mind? What would your life be like if you spent more time with your attention centered at your heart? What if your attention was always heart-centered? Could this simple exercise change your way of living?

More than any other aspect of embodied spirituality, I have found that living more fully from our hearts is *the single most powerful step* for many of us. The shift from thinking of the heart abstractly to actually feeling physical heartbeats can transform us in the moment. Try it when you are already in a fairly present state and let it deepen. Then try it when you are emotionally stuck and see what happens.

Early in an embryo's gestation, the mother's arterial blood enters its body with the rhythm of her pulse rate. That fluid rhythm moves through the body, and cardiac tubes form around it. The heart forms on the basis of the mother's pulse. The heart is a relational structure from its very inception. As the embryo continues to develop, the cardiac tube twists and folds itself into the four chambers of the mature heart.

Those four chambers are composed of multiple layers of spiral muscles. This means that structurally, the heart is relatively complex. Similarly, our ability to feel emotions in the heart is also complex. Our hearts can feel angry and hurt at the same time. Sad and courageous. Terrified and calm. Over time, as we practice feeling our hearts, we can start to notice what emotions are residing there at any given moment. With enough awareness, we can start to feel multiple layers of emotion in our hearts.

2

WISE HEART, EGOIC HEART

When the heart is able to take in all that is presented
in openness, knowledge is able to become wisdom.
—ÉLISABETH ROCHAT DE LA VALLÉE

WHAT ARE EMOTIONS really? We can romanticize
emotions, thinking of them as some sort of poetic
flourish unique to humans. We can reduce them to obscura-
tions of mental clarity. The reality revealed to us through affective neuroscience is that they are essential to life. Fear is the
function of protecting ourselves from danger. Anger is territo-
rial defense. Love is an elaboration of our drive to procreate and
sustain the species. What we call emotion is really the function
of living that has evolved from animal life.

Psychologists have studied emotions for over a hundred years
now. The late nineteenth century saw the emergence of conflicting theories about the origin of emotion from the nascent field
of physiological psychology. Do emotions begin in the mind or
the body? The American psychologist and philosopher William
James and the Danish physician Carl Lange argued, in what
became known as the James-Lange theory of emotion, that
physiological arousal comes first and the experience of emo-

tion second. "The more rational statement is that we feel sorry because we cry, angry because we strike, afraid because we tremble," wrote James, "and not that we cry, strike, or tremble, because we are sorry, angry, or fearful, as the case may be."[2] A generation later, the American physiologist Walter Cannon and his student Philip Bard contended the opposite in the Cannon-Bard theory—that emotional arousal begins in the brain before it resonates in the body.

Now we understand that both are true: waves of overlapping ripples head in both directions, mind-body and body-mind, top-down and bottom-up. The challenge is that with the comforts and complexities of modern life—enduring constant social pressures yet having lots of time on our hands without needing to fulfill survival requirements—these ripples linger in our minds, hearts, and bodies to unnecessary and unhelpful degrees. All of our bodily reactions to our thoughts are predicated on the vivid behavior of animals in the wild. When we become afraid of displeasing the boss, we easily become as physically activated as if there were a bear to run away from. We must learn to recognize, correct, and curtail our confusing thoughts and beliefs—"Nobody likes me. I'm unlucky. I'm doomed to unhappiness. I'll be alone and unloved." Simultaneously we have to complete and release the bodily energy and patterns of emotion that are unspent as there is no bear to run away from.

Emotions are often attended by strong sensations, even overwhelming movements of sensation sweeping through our bodies. If there is a bear to run away from, then we use this energy to run our fastest, careening through the woods with greater agility than if there were no threat. When there is no bear, as our brains recognize the superfluous intensity, they seek to repress it to restore peace and order within our bodies. Ironically, this repression is only partially effective and results in the emotions continuing to persist past their utility. Often, we cognitively fabricate a new reason to be frightened: "Well, there's no bear, but I'm going to be late getting down this mountain." Once we have created a new motivation for the fear, as our emotions persist, we escalate cognitively even further: "If I'm late, my friends are going to be angry." And further: "Really angry. They might never speak to me again." The unspent adrenaline and other physiological responses react to the cognitions in a perfect storm—an ever-enlarging snowball of body-mind escalation.

Commonly, we are taught to downplay emotions—tune them out, repress them, try to rationalize our way out of them. When we find out there is no bear and perhaps not even a lesser danger, if we can calm ourselves down, that is helpful. But what about all the activation in our bodies? The art of working with emotions is being able to express what needs to be expressed and allow emotions to move out of our bodies. Often this takes an active embodiment practice since most of us are so trained in repression. (If you are new to this concept of allowing emotions to move out of the body, you will have lots of opportunity to work with it using the embodiment practices presented in Parts Two and Three of this book.)

And what about spirituality? How do we contextualize our emotions from the point of view of spiritual development? Most spiritual approaches encourage us to tame our emotions, to avoid wallowing or getting swept away. As we become more grounded in sensation, we can take a more challenging but more fruitful path. We can become able to feel emotion, let it move through our bodies, and allow it to transform and expand.

Some emotions refer back to the individual self. They arise because we each have a self, and feeling these emotions reinforces our sense of self, motivates us to understand, protect, and preserve ourselves. I call these *egoic emotions*—sadness, anger, fear, and all their derivatives. Egoic emotions condense us into ourselves and easily convolute into defenses against the environment. Sadness and all its derivatives can move seamlessly into victimization. Anger and its by-products can become aggression. Fear can become withdrawal, aggression, or paralysis.

In contrast, other emotional states are naturally expansive—joy, love, connection, peace, presence. While it *is* possible to twist these expansive emotions too tightly, trying to hoard them as personally affirmative little goodies, they don't easily lend themselves to that purpose. Instead, they can naturally act as bridges into the unitive states, states of connectedness and interdependency, which I call "liberating emotional states."

The complexity of the heart is that we can feel multiple egoic emotions within it at the same time, *and* if we practice emotional heart awareness, there can be an ongoing, simultaneous backdrop of liberating emotional states—wisdom, peace, and presence! Finally, as we become skilled in this practice, we can allow egoic emotions to transform into liberating states.

The first step is recognizing the wise heart.

Discovering the Wise Heart

Take a few moments to center in yourself. Feel your body and its sensations. Become aware of how you are breathing. Notice if there are any important physical or emotional issues that need attention.

When you feel ready, think of a big question, developmental challenge, or dilemma in your life right now. As you bring this to mind, see how your body responds to the thought. Notice the sensations of your response and the shape of the gesture they form.

Acknowledging that, settle back into your whole self. Ask your heart, "Can you help me with these feelings?" Feel the subtle shifts that arise in response to that question. Let your whole being settle into the feeling of having your heart embrace and support the thought you introduced.

Ask yourself what wisdom or truth your heart is offering you at this moment. Wait until words form.

I did this inside myself as I wrote it. I thought of a dilemma with one of my family members, how to support them during a big, scary transition in their life. Very subtly, I felt the front of my heart draw together and up, a little grasping gesture, an expression of concern. This feeling extended from my heart up into my throat and face as well. These feelings were an egoic emotional mix of fear, sadness, and concern. When I asked my heart to lovingly hold those feelings, I felt my whole heart spread out in all directions, as if opening its arms to the smaller emotions. I let the two types of feeling rest together for a while. I asked for words to describe the message coming from my heart of wisdom: "It's going to be okay. Love, wait, rest."

As we practice feeling our hearts over time, the relationship between our wise hearts and our emotional hearts can clarify and become more articulate. Check in as often as you want. How is your heart feeling? Check with all the parts of your heart that you can identify. Try feeling the front of your heart, the center of your heart, the top of your heart, the bottom, and the sides.

The back of the heart is connected to the spine via a fairly thick layer of connective tissue. This tissue does not have a lot of sensory nerve endings or blood supply. It is quiet without a lot of sensation. In this way, the back of the heart is a place where we can tuck away emotions we don't wish to deal with. And we can forget about them for indefinitely long periods of time until something intensifies.

The top of the heart is directly involved in our throats, speech, and facial expressions. We sometimes practice pushing down on the top of our hearts, repressing that part so as not to reveal ourselves to the world. Taking the lid off the top of the heart can be a joyful relief. Opening the top of our hearts is often associated with lightheartedness.

Checking in with our hearts and clearing any emotional dilemmas can become a daily practice, individually and relationally. This was prescribed in Chinese medicine as early as 500 B.C.E., in the time of Confucius. Here is a description of the heart and heart practice from the "Neiye," or "Inner Training," chapter of the *Guanzi*, an ancient Chinese philosophical text:

> When our Hearts are well regulated, our senses are
>   well regulated too.
> When our Hearts are at rest, our sense organs are at
>   rest too.
> What regulates them is the Heart.
> What sets them at rest is the Heart.
> (That is to say) within the Heart there is another
>   Heart.
> The art of the heart is to empty the heart every day.[3]

On a personal level, what actions do you need to take so that your heart can open and relax? Relationally, what do you need to communicate with others to relieve your heart of any worries each day?

Of course, we must also clear any dilemmas in the rest of our beings as well. If our bodies or brains build up too much stress, we are not able to fully support our hearts. We constrict the full circulation of our hearts. Feel what physical and emotional changes you can begin to make, so that eventually your body becomes a living throne for the relaxed majesty of your heart.

In this way, we clear our bodies to support the heart. And we clear our hearts so they can shine like the sun!

Sophia,[4] a twenty-something student of embodied spirituality, contacted me, distraught about a recent breakup. I had always been impressed by her unique combination of innocence and wisdom. Now she was sobbing, barely able to speak through the pain. I sat with her, feeling my own heart aching for her and with her. At the same time, around the ache, my heart felt big and expansive, calm, with a deep knowing that she would not only survive this loss, but grow and thrive by learning from it. This was my heart of wisdom holding the space for both of our emotions.

When Sophia was finished crying, I suggested she feel her body. She felt her heart was the center of the strongest sensations. There she felt a swirl of conflicting emotions—anger, pain, confusion. She wasn't eating or sleeping well and not performing well at her job. She experienced her heart as betrayed and betraying, untrustworthy in that it had led her into yet another disastrous relationship. When she recognized that this was her small, emotional heart, she settled down and felt more deeply, looking for the wiser, bigger heart of awareness. As she rested into the sensations of her chest, she felt something open deep inside, "as if the clouds parted and my chest was suddenly open and full of light, clarity." From this place, she realized that her ex was lost in confusion, unavailable for a real relationship.

As we talked through all this and she continued to feel her heart and her body, she allowed many parts of herself to communicate with each other. She felt relaxed and trusting of herself and her ability to be by herself for a while, without rushing into the next relationship. She felt she could touch back into her body awareness, and particularly her heart, over the next days and weeks as this process evolved within her. A deeper commitment emerged to check in with her heart's wisdom the next time she felt curious about exploring intimacy. Now she could soothe all those disturbing emotions just by staying present with this larger heart awareness.

3

THE WISDOM OF EMOTIONS

WHEN I WAS growing up in the southern United States in the 1960s, Jim Crow segregation laws strongly affected everyone's lives. I went to a church where everyone was very white in looks and behavior. Everyone spoke in hushed voices. Their faces were either neutral or held a faint smile. The women held their purses and limbs very close in and admonished the children to do likewise. The men had a couple of inches of greater leeway for movement, but not that much. As I remember it, I was uncomfortable with all this feeling of life and emotion being so tightly contained. I also remember being uncomfortable because I was darker than anyone else there.

In contrast, when I happened to go past black churches during Sunday service, I was mesmerized. Wow, so much noise, movement, music, interaction! So much emotion! I wanted to go in so badly, but I wasn't dark enough to go in without disrupting what was happening. Those memories have stayed with me all these years. I was a bit too dark for one church, but it was too contained for me. And I was too light for the other. Although the racial dimension of these experiences is important, it's not my focus here. The key is the difference in emotional expressivity, but the general pattern was not lost on me as a child.

Remembering this helped me understand why I had to leave that church I grew up in, and these memories helped me envision the possibility of embodied spirituality.

EMOTIONAL EXPRESSION, REPRESSION, AND HABITUATION

In animals, behavior and emotion are relatively continuous. In the study of affective neuroscience, we see that fundamental behaviors such as territory defense and food seeking are the basis of human emotions.[5] Even when there is nothing tangible to protect, we humans may experience fear. Even when all our needs are met, we often experience desire. Beyond manifesting behavioral tendencies as emotion, the human brain is able to pick and choose how it manifests emotion. The unique ability of the adult human brain is the possibility of expressing or repressing emotions. Over the course of our lifetimes, we create a personality structure of rehearsed repertoires of emotional expression and repression.

In his concept of *repetition compulsion,* Sigmund Freud helped us start to understand how much of our behavior is acting out unconscious emotional patterns. This is the most blatant arena of ego activity. Our egos are these habitual patterns and our identification with them—"I am this kind of person who behaves and feels these ways" over and over again. Many of us will pursue this kind of activity until it kills us, literally. This is the conditioned self that has wrapped its web around the true self and true nature. Our bodies are the clay that is molded by our habitual behavior and our conditioned concepts of ourselves, and there are layers and layers of this.

Awareness in the moment brings us into direct contact with what we are doing and feeling and thinking now. Contemplating our lives over time allows us to see the patterns. Are we always in the role of victim, aggressor, or bystander? What are our beliefs about who we are? About what the world is? What do we identify as "me"? When did we learn these patterns? How do we reinforce them? What postures do our hearts take to support these stances and attachments? All of this has been relegated to the realm of psychology and therapy, but clearly it is the structure of the ego and, therefore, the path of moving through our habitual emotional patterns. These are part of the conditioned self. As we let these habitual patterns unwind, we move toward the true self and true nature. In this way, emotional awareness and unwinding habitual pattern are the substance of any spiritual path. Through emotional awareness, habitual patterns unwind. This is liberation.

Some people see the spiritual path almost as a random egoic demolition process. Just smash the hell out of that thing called ego! Get rid of it as quickly as you can! Sadly, it seems that you have to be pretty evolved for this kind of approach to be helpful. Otherwise, it just makes you crazy.

Habitual patterns are not just the trappings of ego, they are also the ground of our everyday sanity. It is a good thing that we get up every morning and clothe and feed ourselves. How can we examine our patterns, discern what is working optimally and what is no longer functional? How can we sort through what to accept and what to work through? How can we work with ourselves with love and awareness to blossom in our fullest potential, shedding the old patterns gently yet courageously?

For most of us, this deep level of growth and change is a very slow process. As Arnold Mindell, the founder of process-oriented psychology, said to me once, "We change so slowly, but there's so much richness in the circling, don't you think?" The main point here is to be gentle and gracious with ourselves.

There is utility in seeing the continuity between our personal psychological and emotional growth and our spiritual development. It is a continuum. As Thomas Hora said, "All problems are psychological and all solutions are spiritual."[6] Working through all these layers seems to be a slow process indeed.

If we allow an organic continuity between our habitual ways and our becoming, we can enter any emotionally challenging experience and let it mold us, melt us, and ultimately transform us. The new person may only be subtly different than the one that began the process. Appreciating those subtleties then becomes the next step on the path and an essential step in the transformational process. If we miss the baby steps, then we may never take any giant leaps. By holding an awareness of our psychological work as an essential part of our spiritual paths, we potentiate both psychological and spiritual development. Without this awareness, psychological work can become unnaturally encapsulated in a small-minded, egotistical fixation on the self. Spiritual work can become unrealistically lofty and idealized.

EMOTIONAL WISDOM

Anxiety is excitement without the breath.
—ALEXANDER LOWEN

In some philosophies, emotions exist in a continuum, spanning the spectrum from confusion to wisdom. For example, fear is related to both courage and peace. Anger can transform into clarity and creativity. In Chinese medicine, each emotional essence is paired with an element. The earth element is negatively associated with the rejection of relationship, but its transformative features are centeredness, connection, and richness. The metal element is associated with rigidity and isolation, which transform into inspiration and openness. The fire element's challenge is coldness and seriousness, while its positive quality is joy and laughter. By examining these pairs, we glimpse the possibility of emotional morasses transforming into wisdom.

Some approaches to Buddhism share this transformational view of emotion. Vajrayana Buddhism is literally translated as the "indestructible path." Indestructible because nothing need be discarded. Through practicing mindful presence continuously and fully, anger is transformed into mirrorlike wisdom. Ignorance transforms into nonconceptual wisdom. Poverty transforms into appreciation and equanimity. Clinging transforms into discernment. Competitiveness becomes skillful action. Again, we are mining the potential that is inherent in the challenge. By practicing presence fully and deeply, we become able to open so fully that transformation naturally occurs.

Take a moment and check in with yourself. Are there any emotions clearly arising in you right now? If so, pause and feel them in your body. If not, remember the last time you felt some strong emotions arise. See if, as you remember, you can feel the presence of the emotion in your body. Notice where in your body the emotion is present. What are the sensations of this emotion? Give yourself the time to just be with whatever you are feeling. Take an attitude of kindness and patience toward what you are feeling. Sit with the feeling in this atmosphere of patience and kindness. Let yourself breathe. Watch as the sensations shift within you. As you repeat this process, your ability to breathe and allow your whole being to shift and resolve will increase. The irony is that if we go in seeking transformation, the changes will not happen. If we enter with an open, accepting mind and heart, then we can ask ourselves, "What is the wisdom of this emotion?" This will enable us to move in that direction. As we continue through this book, we will learn and discover for ourselves details that can expedite this process, but cultivating patience and kindness for ourselves is a bottom line.

As our emotions transform, not only do we feel better within ourselves, but our relationship to the world around us becomes clearer and more direct. We can better distinguish between our ideas and our actual experience. Out of this, we can better discern what we are actually perceiving, instead of being caught up in our mental constructs and projections. This is helpful in working with ourselves, but it is essential in relating to others. When we are not clear about our own experience, we often project the unconscious aspects of ourselves onto others. Working with our own emotions is the basis for working with others. Knowing what we are feeling in our hearts and bodies from moment to moment is the basis for working with emotions.

In our culture, which is so individualistic, disembodied, and disconnected from wild nature, those of us who want to access the wisdom of our emotions need to practice doing so. When emotions are overwhelming, the intention is to ground in the body without repressing the process. Emotions come in waves. Learn to let them wash over you without smashing you. The wash of emotions can let us sort out the clarity from the confusion, the love from the fear. And once again, we begin with the path and practice of the heart.

4

A PATH OF LOVE

The body is the ultimate witness to love.
—OCEAN VUONG, *ON BEING* INTERVIEW

IN THE PREVIOUS chapters, we explored the centrality of the heart to both physiology and emotion. With its powerful electromagnetic field, the heart sets the tone for our whole state of being. The heart entrances all of our cells into a particular mind state. In fact, physicists have shown that the strongest electromagnetic field entrains all the fields with which it interacts. What is more, cellular biology teaches us that the integral proteins in the cell membranes change their shape in response to the electromagnetic information in their field. The heart is the drummer to whose rhythm the cells dance.

What does the heart communicate to the cells? Many different kinds of messages. But when the heart is open and resting in its truest and deepest expression, we could call its message peace, awareness, life, presence, or love.

Resting in Open Heart

Take a moment and rest your whole body, your whole being. With each exhalation, drop deeper into a state of rest. Invite your mind to rest its thinking into awareness of breath and sensation. Scan through your body and let it relax into a comfortable position wherever you are. Let all muscles—internal and external, skeletal and visceral—relax, lengthen, and let go. Feel the sense that all of you is present.

From this place, check in with your heart. Feel any currents of emotion that are there. Acknowledge them; feel them; let them move, breathe; and, as much as possible, release them. Let them clear from your heart just as the clouds part and the mist burns away, so the sun can shine clear and bright in the sky.

Resting now with a clear and open heart, notice how the sensations in your chest feel. Are the sensations confined to the center of your chest where your heart resides? Do they seem to radiate out, like the heart's field? When our hearts are open fully, the boundaries of physicality soften, lighten, and even dissolve.

Let your open heart energy radiate out as far as it goes. Does it fill the room? Can it connect out to the sky? Beyond?

The open heart takes us beyond a feeling of small self into a sense of continuity with the world.

Leading with Heart

I hope this practice allowed you to experience the expansiveness of the heart's energy. Doing so even in a quiet room and with guidance can be difficult, never mind as we go about our busy lives. The question remains—how do we integrate our hearts into our daily lives?

Practice heart meditation every day or as often as you are able. Do it right now, even for a moment. I know we just did it a moment ago, but that's the thing about practice—it's all about repetition. Rest as deeply as possible into your heartbeat (again, do it right now!) in your meditation and then see how long you can continue that awareness as you transition into activity. The more you rest into pulsation, the more quickly you can make the shift from a solid, ego-driven state to a fluid, universal state. If you practice often enough, it is possible to drop into the pulsation with a moment's intention.

Watch over time as your heart awareness pops up during life activities. The more frequently and deeply you practice, the more frequently your heart awareness will come to you spontaneously in the midst of your life.

Remember your heart whenever you are able. Remember your heart in moments of emotion.

When you are in a state of joy, it is a good time to feel the continuity between your heart, your whole body, and the space around you.

When you are in a state of sorrow, it might take some time to feel your heart under the heaviness in your chest. Take the time to excavate it. This is not about getting rid of the sadness or the heaviness, but looking for the essence of the heart amid the rubble of thoughts and emotions, to find the sensations and pulsations of the heart itself.

When you are in a state of anger, the push and activation of anger is so loud, it easily masks the subtlety of the heart itself, like looking for a quiet sage in the midst of a busy marketplace. Look, look again, and keep looking until you can find your heart and rest. What has happened to the anger then?

When you are frightened and cringing, or quiet and still, how can your heart soothe you and give you courage at the same time?

When you are frightened and frantic, and your heart is beating hard and fast, look for the wise, calm heart within the fear, perhaps at the center of it all. When you can find it and stay with it for a while, where is the fear?

Remember your heart in your interactions with others. Notice how quickly you shift from openheartedness to some kind of self-centered position. Imagine someone you know approaching, clearly wanting something from you. Imagine someone saying, "I am disappointed in our interaction." In each case, what happens to your heart, and what happens if you shift into an open heart?

ATTACHMENT AND OPENNESS

So much of our practice is noticing the fluctuation of attachment and openness in the sensations in our chests and hearts. Attachment often has a hallmark of tension, grasping, holding the energy in these areas; whereas openness is and feels open.

I am in the middle of a dilemma in my own heart. I am so attached to the beauty of our planet. As I write this, it is spring, and the new green of the leaves feeds me so deeply that I want to explode into blossom. The birds dance an invitation around me. The rain soothes me to the bone. I also feel so attached to all humans. It's not just that I love my friends and family, my students and my community. I am deeply, deeply attached to the idea of the human species finding a way to live sustainably on the earth. I want the planet to continue to unfurl and evolve in a healthy, sustainable way. And I want humanity to be a part of that. If I hold these two attachments too tightly, too closely, with too little awareness, a conflict develops between them. It's so much to want and seems like such an incomprehensible stretch that we can get there. That conflict manifests in my heart as a tightening of fear and aggression. Without attention, I spin into an agitated, negative state. With time and repeated attention, I can let this resolve. The sensations of tension around my heart dissolve, and I can think in a more open, accepting way: what will be will be. I shift from attached clinging, pushing both sides of the conflict, to a feeling of love. I love this planet of ours. And I love us.

Feeling the natural fluctuations of our attachment and openness can give us a sense of patience with ourselves. We can give up the task of trying to be spiritually correct and be simply and humbly with what is.

PRACTICING LOVE

Emotional awareness of the heart generally requires quiet meditative time to develop, especially when one is fairly new to the practice. As emotional heart awareness develops, you can challenge yourself to renew that awareness in more varied and active situations. Remember your heart as you contemplate the world. As you form opinions, make decisions, read the news, decide how to vote—in all of these, feel your heart. What feels right in your heart? Get to know the quiet feelings of unrest that might signal a sense of disharmony with a situation or decision. This is not a clear, loud voice coming down from the heavens, infallibly directing you: "YES, THAT IS THE CORRECT CHOICE." Instead it is a quiet, subtle sense: "That feels right," or "Hm, that doesn't feel exactly right."

The more we listen—quietly, humbly, openly—the more we hear. The more we hear, the more we can lead with the heart. The more we lead with the heart, the more we find that we are resting not only in pulsation and awareness, but in love itself.

Opening our hearts allows us to lead with our hearts. Leading with our hearts is not the impulsive rush for personal love with which we have been culturally indoctrinated. That is leading with the small heart and pursuing the smallest version of love. The wise heart naturally considers the well-being of the collective. The wise heart exudes love without regard for self-gain. It seems to create an atmosphere of love, but perhaps it is merely tuning us in to the field of love that is the ground of our universe.

The Physiology of Compassion

Even as I use grandiose terms like "field of love," what I'm talking about is not separate from the simple, physical reality of our bodies. As we shall see throughout this book, spiritual qualities emerge on a physical level as we become ever more familiar with our own bodily systems and their inner and outer relationships. As we become more mindful of the here and now, our brain function becomes more cohesive and complete, and there is more flow as the information of sensation smoothly reaches our brains from our peripheral nerves. We process the incoming information more simply and directly. Our cognition proceeds through our brain centers more elegantly, and speech, movement, and behavior flow out in a more organized manner.

The rest of our systems rest more neutrally and move more

effortlessly. Finally, and most importantly, our hearts are open muscularly and vascularly. Our lungs are relaxed and working with our hearts in a harmonious manner. Our diaphragms and throats are relaxed and relatively open to allow our heart energy free rein throughout our bodies. These quite physical processes have everything to do with how we show up in our relationships and in the world—that is, with how much compassion flows through us and out into our lives.

Practice feeling your heart. The great gift of embodied spirituality is that we can begin with something tangible, in this case, the sensations in the chest area, and let that lead us to spirit. Practice releasing your heart into its natural expansiveness. It is less that we actively open our hearts than that we allow them their natural blossoming. Spend time with your emotional dilemmas until they dissolve on their own. Then let the boundaries of your heart dissolve as well.

Many approaches to spirituality include some kind of spiritual fruition—realization, enlightenment, liberation, union with God. In Buddhism it is said that all of our true nature is open and clear, like a blue sky, completely free of clouds. Of course, in this metaphor the clouds represent our confused, egoic minds. We all know the joy of a sunny day, a blessing of expansiveness. When rain comes after a dry period, that too is a blessing. In embodied spirituality we strive to host the open heart and the cloudy heart with equal graciousness.

When approached with sincerity, the first gift of embodiment practices is the shift toward feeling what is, even if it is confusion, pain, suffering, or discomfort. Over time, as we practice opening to sensation, feeling our bodies more deeply and fully, we develop greater skill in discerning how to be with challenging emotions and sensations. Sometimes we can focus on the sensations of the emotion. Other times, we need to give ourselves a larger context, to feel our whole bodies and areas of less intensity as a way of offering the emotions a larger or deeper support. As this discernment grows, we can experience the bliss of an open heart more deeply, and even the suffering or confused heart can be appreciated as its own type of grace.

This is why we devote so much time to feeling, the second step of embodied spirituality and the focus of our next section, in which we will explore the body in all its depth and glory. Now, to gain sustenance for that journey, pause once again. Feel your heart in all its fullness and pulsation. Let your heart shine like the sun. Let your heart's radiance dissolve the boundaries—its own and those of your whole body. Feel this heart, this body, this center, to be the center of a vast field of love.

How might we change the world by opening our hearts?

PART TWO
Body of Life

5

ONE WITH THE WORLD: EVOLUTION AND ANIMALITY

· ·

> Space is not empty. It is full, a plenum as opposed
> to a vacuum, and is the ground for the existence
> of everything, including ourselves. The universe is
> not separate from this cosmic sea of energy.
> —DAVID BOHM

WHERE DID WE come from, we humans, with our beautiful hearts that can open so expansively into an awareness of the universe? In the largest sense, the answer is ultimately a mystery, but we can learn a great deal by looking back into our evolutionary legacy. We are humans. We are hominids. We are mammals. We are animals. We are living creatures. We are a part of this glorious biosphere called earth. What can we learn by studying our nature at each of those levels? What is unique and fundamental about being human? What is true for all mammals? And how is all this relevant to embodied spirituality? These are the questions we'll be exploring in this brief chapter, which provides some conceptual grounding that we will use in subsequent chapters as we explore step two of embodied spirituality, feeling your body.

For more than two million years, our most immediate ancestors, hominids of the *Homo sapiens* species, wandered the earth. They mostly grouped in packs of twenty to forty, living by means of hunting and gathering. About two hundred thousand years ago, the subspecies *Homo sapiens sapiens* emerged. This is who we are, *our* subspecies—the modern human. We evolved out of the hunting and gathering lifestyle practiced by all the hominids before us, and the resources and challenges of that lifestyle shaped our modern abilities. Thinking about seasonal patterns and migration behavior seems to have stretched our brains. Tracking animals and foraging for food developed our eye-hand coordination and our agility. The need to pass on our learning required more articulate hands and mouths. Yet even after this most modern version of humans emerged, we continued to live as hunters and gatherers for about 190,000 years.

Ten thousand years ago, a cultural inflection point occurred. Nothing changed in our physical beings. Humans seem to have basically the same skeletal structures, brain size, genetic composition today as they did two hundred thousand years ago and ten thousand years ago. The physiology remained the same, but a mere ten thousand years ago, some of us started living differently, practicing the most primitive forms of agriculture—gathering seeds and casting them out onto untilled soil. Shortly thereafter, some of us began to shepherd animals and, a bit later, settle down in more permanent dwellings. At this point, culture itself began to burgeon. Our artistry expanded in all media. We have records of visual art. We can only imagine what might have been born musically and in language. We have flutes and drums from forty thousand years ago and lyres from three thousand years ago. Storytelling evolved into mythology

and political oration. The meter of change gradually acceler-
ated. And it continued to accelerate, until this ever-changing
now in which we live, a state in which everything is evolving
so quickly that the change feels constant. A near singularity of
cultural change!

While the cultural change is huge, the physical evolution is
minimal. Thus, on a physical level, everything we think of as
human—from higher order cognition, language, and tool development to living with and caring for each other in our uniquely
human way—evolved during our millions of years as hunters
and gatherers. So, although it is far more common nowadays
to talk about our hearts and bodies in modern psychological
terms, it is important to understand that they are also the precious result of nearly unfathomable spans of evolutionary development. Learning to deepen our felt embodiment is a return to
billions of years of natural intelligence.

Our Animal Bodies
and the Unitive State

If you study animals, you see that, for the most part, they are
very relaxed. Think of a cow lying in a field, looking out into
space. Her mind seems open and resting in the present moment,
not preoccupied with past and future thoughts—looking out
without seeming to focus on anything in particular. Cows are
great meditators!

Even in the wild, even when hunting, hunted, or hungry,
most animals are not whipping themselves into a neurological
frenzy or stuck in some mental-emotional bog. They are calm
enough to bring their whole being into alertness. This open,
relaxed alertness, which we could also simply call awareness, is

the basis of what we humans, whether two hundred thousand years ago or today, experience as meditation.

Hunting and gathering humans still exist on our planet in remote parts of Africa, Indonesia, and the Amazon. They are evidently creative and intelligent, and they still embody this relaxed openness. Sitting quietly, they easily slip into meditative states. Of course, this stillness is punctuated by all sorts of activity and emotionality, but it seems that quietude is a baseline with which we "civilized" humans have lost touch.

Within this relaxed, open state, there is connectedness. Hunters and gatherers are deeply embedded in their world, at one with it. Whether we conceive of this as union with the spirits, God, the great spirit, the earth, or compassionate awareness, the neurophysiological state is the same. There is a family of related and overlapping states that we could call *unitive*. We experience these as a vast continuity. People in the unitive state still feel conscious of themselves to greater or lesser degrees. On the "lesser" end of the spectrum, we can experience states such as trances or deep meditative absorption. When we are more conscious of ourselves while in the unitive state, however, we experience ourselves as centered within "all that is." This means when we are not busy maintaining awareness of ourselves as separate from all that is, then there is just a field of awareness, love, continuity—without a center or fringe.

In industrialized, technological cultures, most of us have lost this deep sense of unity. Some of us devote ourselves to rediscovering it through meditation, contemplation, prayer, devotion, nature, and community. The following is a part of a message from a culture still rooted in the unitive state, the Kogi people. The Kogi live in the Sierra Nevada in Santa Marta in Colombia. They write here to the rest of humanity, calling to us as their younger brothers:

From the Heart of the World:
The Elder Brothers Warning

The Great Mother created the world in water. She makes the future in it. This is how she speaks to us. We look after nature. We are the mámas and do this here. And we mámas see that you are killing it by what you do. We can no longer repair the world. You must. You are uprooting the earth. And we are divining to discover how to teach you to stop.[7]

Though the Kogi are not purely hunters and gatherers, they are still living embedded in nature, as we all did for such a long period of time. Only in these last few thousand years have we created a serious rupture between ourselves and nature. The Kogi are calling on us, the younger brothers, to wake up to the havoc we are reaping on our mother earth. When we lose contact with the unitive state, we don't notice that we are doing harm. We don't notice the rupture, but we identify with the results. We feel forsaken by God. Many of us feel like isolated little people within a big universe. Or worse, we are obsessed with our own self-importance, ignoring all else. We become trapped in our egos, without a direct link to others. At this point, compassion becomes a mental exercise at best or is forgotten at worst.

We've already discussed the cultural inflection point of ten thousand years ago. As that cultural momentum surged, we became less connected to nature and probably more confused as to our place in the world. Organized, institutional religions emerged about three thousand years ago. Was their emergence at least partly in response to the rupture of connection, an attempt to repair it? Are religion and spirituality attempts to reconnect to our birthright, our ability to rest in meditative and unitive states?

Modern life is terribly stimulating and fast-paced. At times, it rides us like a mad demon. We are bombarded and distracted away from spiritual states. Yet, though we may be largely unaware of it, the drive toward spirituality is deep and innate within our physiology. It is a drive toward coming home. It doesn't go away, it just becomes obscured. We find ourselves avoiding meditation, religion, prayer, yoga—anything that might lead us back to it. Our nervous systems don't want us to let our guard down, to shift gears into a more open state.

Our nervous systems are in large part protective defense structures, committed to maintaining homeostasis. If they have been functioning safely within a narrow scope of awareness, then they have to be seduced into opening outward. Once we have a taste of a larger consciousness, then we have to ascertain that it is safe.

However, despite this resistance, most people have moments when they stumble into the sacred world. Whether it is cresting a mountain, making love, flying a plane, holding a baby—most of us have moments where everything opens up. There's a stillness, a presence, a luminosity. Our hearts open. We feel full, and we let go of our striving. We are content; we are at one with our world. Yet if we leave such experiences to chance, if we fail to appreciate, study, cultivate, and practice them, then it is all too likely that they will become fleeting in our lives as we get more and more habituated to the disembodied norms of modern life.

Thankfully there is an ancient, tried-and-tested method for learning this fluency—the practice of mindfulness of the body. I

teach this practice in an adapted form, encouraging more movement and expression than is traditional in many spiritual contexts. This practice manifests the spiral quality of the steps of
embodied spirituality: out of the aspiration to open our hearts,
we may commit to a practice of mindfully feeling our bodies;
and as we move more fully into feeling our bodies, we begin to
trust our bodies to express themselves more. This is the step of
allowing. As we allow the sensations in our bodies to express
themselves more fully, we may find that our hearts have begun
to open of their own accord. At each stage, our connections
with ourselves and the rest of the world deepen and blossom.

6

THE CENTER OF HERE, THE CENTER OF NOW: MINDFULNESS OF BODY

This very body that we have, that's sitting right here right
now . . . with its aches and its pleasures . . . is exactly what
we need to be fully human, fully awake, fully alive.

—PEMA CHÖDRÖN

WHEN WE ARE living in a body, that body is the center of here and the center of now.

The *Satipatthana Sutra*, or *Discourse on the Establishing of Mindfulness*, is the first recorded mention of the idea of mindfulness as we know it today. Mindfulness is the cornerstone of all Buddhist approaches to meditation and has spread into virtually all aspects of contemporary health and wellness culture. In this sutra, Shakyamuni Buddha presents the Four Foundations of Mindfulness. They are, in the most common iteration, mindfulness of body, mindfulness of feeling, mindfulness of mind, and mindfulness of phenomena.

FOUR FOUNDATIONS OF MINDFULNESS	
1.	Mindfulness of body
2.	Mindfulness of feeling
3.	Mindfulness of mind
4.	Mindfulness of phenomena

Animals, as usual, furnish perfect examples of effortless, unwavering mindfulness of body and phenomena. Where we differ, as humans, is in our uniquely acute ability to recognize that we have a mind, and ultimately—through mindfulness of mind—to transform the experience of our minds from egocentric small-mindedness to open, all-encompassing awareness of *what is*.

Conversely, as humans, we also have a uniquely acute ability to imagine *what is not*. This is our wonderful creativity and allows us to make art, build bridges, and go to the moon. For most of us, on a daily basis, this creativity runs away from the moment and ties us up in knots of conjecture, self-consciousness, and hatred.

This ability to imagine resides primarily in the frontal lobe of our cerebral cortex, one of the parts of ourselves that became larger and more complex than the frontal lobes of not only other mammals but even earlier subspecies of humans, such as *Homo habilis* and *Homo neanderthalensis*.

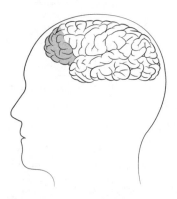

Frontal lobe of the cerebral cortex

Our frontal lobes are involved not only in creative thinking but also in conscious thought, higher order cognition, and executive function. When we allow the frontal cortex to run the show, to tell the rest of the body what to do, this is referred to in neuropsychology as "top-down functioning." When more ancient brain structures and the rest of our bodies initiate our behavior, we call this "bottom-up functioning."

At this point in history, most human cultures are dominated by top-down functioning. We assert control over our behavior, our bodies, and our lives based on our ideas about the right way to live, the right way to be. Some positive outcomes of this way of functioning are reflection, understanding, and wisdom. When top-down functioning is relied on to the exclusion of bottom-up functioning, however, our bodies become mere interruptions, symptoms to be managed, machines to be maintained. The earth becomes a resource to be exploited, rather than a mother to be revered.

In contrast, when we practice mindfulness of body, we listen to our sensations, and that listening becomes the basis for strengthening our bottom-up functioning. We move toward a balance of top-down and bottom-up functioning—a healthy, creative partnership between all aspects of body, heart, and mind. This begins with listening to sensations. Sensations are the language of the body. Since most of us have not done a lot of listening to our sensations, our brains have learned a strategy of muting sensation. We habitually operate in a "sleep" mode of sorts that tells the body to be quiet and not disrupt our intended activities.

RECLAIMING OUR SENSATIONS

There is an antidote to our modern habit of shutting our bodies down. It is mindfulness of body—the practice of feeling the sensations that are arising in our bodies right now.

Sensations are physiology occurring in the body in this present moment: muscles shortening, fluids circulating, chemicals accumulating, and myriad other processes. Sensations have an emotional tone, a quality of feeling (the second foundation of mindfulness), associated with either well-being or distress, living or dying. That emotional tone sometimes blossoms into full-blown emotions. Anger, joy, grief, love, and every possible variation of human attitude toward experience is felt in the body as sensation.

In mindfulness practice we feel the sensations in our bodies now—not "now" in any abstract sense but *right now*. However, a further step is required. As mentioned, in our habit of privileging and relying on top-down functioning, we have shut down some of our basic physiology. We have directed ourselves not to move, not to breathe in certain ways, not to feel. We do this both consciously and unconsciously. Most of us know the feeling of trying not to laugh or cry. Some of us are acutely aware of working to hold ourselves still, to stay focused in a polite manner. These repressions filter down to all aspects of our physiology—into our muscles, heart function, brain function, digestion—all cellular function. They even affect our genetic expression. They become habitualized in our physiology. This is the intricate training of "civilized" humanity. We have trained ourselves, in some small degree, out of life and into a less animate state. Obviously, these kinds of physiological repression filter differently through different cultures, even though they affect everyone. In recent years, oppressed and marginalized people have been finding ways to express more about how constricted they feel when moving in spaces dominated by other groups. In addition, as I found as a child in relation to white and black churches, some racial cultures seem to support expression in a generalized way more than others do. Then there is the cultural oppression arising from social prejudices regarding gender, sexual preference, and many other identity markers. Here again, there are the constraints of expression, movement, and behavior that become so internalized that we may explore our own embodiment and never excavate their deeper layers. So, in embodiment work, we are not only exploring our personal and familial learning of constriction but also that caused by myriad cultural oppressions.

Although it is beyond the scope of this book, I would feel remiss if I left this discussion without acknowledging that constriction is just the most benign manifestation of cultural oppression, its earliest footprint. That constriction snowballs into trauma, violence, disease, death, and every type of social issue. Recognizing all this, we can only hope that our practice of embodied spirituality can ripple out and support social change. At the very least, I can attest that as my sensitivity increases, it increases my motivation to do whatever I can to work toward social justice.

To counteract this, we need to go beyond mindfulness of sensation. We need to allow our physiology to restart itself where it has been slowed down. To live fully again, we must practice allowing what we have silenced and held still. We begin with mindfulness of body, and then, in my approach to embodied spirituality, we give the sensations we feel permission to move, to rest, to breathe, to sound, and to speak in their own way. By going slowly and gently, we can find safe ways to reintegrate parts of ourselves that we have shut down. In my work, I call this Embodiment Practice. We'll begin exploring the details of this practice in the next several chapters. In Part Three of this book, I'll give you pithy instructions for your own practice, and we'll explore the development of Embodiment Practice more fully. For now, let's continue to lay the groundwork.

Listening to and Allowing Sensations

Although most of us have lost touch with our embodiment as adults due to our continuous efforts to control, edit, and truncate our breath, movement, behavior, and words, there is no shortage of embodiment models for us to follow. For the most part, all other creatures on the planet are fully embodied all the time. Human babies and children are generally quite embodied. As noted in the introduction to this book, we can define embodiment as the continuous, complete, and free flow of cognition, emotion, and behavior through our bodies.

Embodiment Practice begins with the mindful listening to sensation and adds permission to shift out of the top-down dominion of the brain as leader into a self-directed, body-based way of being. We extend our listening to sensations by allowing the sensations to live more fully and freely.

Since sensations are physiology—electrochemical, biomechanical activity—they move in space. Muscles shortening and lengthening move us in an obvious manner. The peristalsis of our digestive processes involves the internal movement of rhythmic contractions and the external movement toward food, rest, or just a postural shift. Our perceptive processes move us toward and away from objects and other beings. On a cellular level, there are busy subcellular organelles bustling around inside each cell at all times. In any given moment, the sum total of all our sensations comes together and naturally sequences our behavior. This is always occurring, from the cellular inner gestures of physiology to the gross visible movements of the body and all the way to emotional expression and communication. Sensation can lead us to lie down, to jump, to extend a hand, to fall in love, to start a war. Everything we do—all movements, states, and behaviors—has its foundation in sensation.

Although there are techniques, such as many forms of meditation, in which we practice mindfulness of the body in stillness, in Embodiment Practice as I teach it, we do not just listen to sensation by keeping our bodies still. The reason is that people too often experience stillness as muteness and submissiveness. Instead, we listen and allow whatever we feel to move and breathe *in its own way*. This is an innate ability, something all animals do almost all the time. We can reawaken this ability, but it takes some degree of intention, practice, and often time.

Laura's presence in a group always commanded a lot of attention, because she was so very still. Also extremely quiet, she never spoke unless it was necessary. Most of her Embodiment Practice was similarly still and quiet, very internal. She attended a number of workshops and retreats over the years. We came to know each other almost subliminally. As her embodiment emerged, it remained quiet and subtle. At a certain point, however, there was a distinct blossoming. I suspected a deep healing, but I never asked, and confirmation was never offered. After a period of time, I realized that her presence was no longer so striking. The stillness and silence had softened. There was no longer an alarming undertone. There was gentle movement and some quiet comments that seemed to flow organically, like a tiny spring that bubbled up from the earth.

In meditation, the goal is to arrive at this kind of dynamic stillness. Often, we hold ourselves still when we meditate. I have personally spent a lot of time meditating with a held stillness. However, as I began to feel confidence in the idea of embodied spirituality, I began allowing more movement in meditation— not in a frivolous way, but through small movements that felt like a vital unwinding of my physiology and emotions. By allowing movement when it felt "necessary," I found myself arriving at a dynamic, authentic state of stillness more quickly than when I was imposing a held stillness on my practice.

There is a powerful relationship between movement and stillness. They are two sides of the same phenomenon. Embodied spirituality is based on the experience that cultivating movement allows dynamic stillness to unfold more deeply and readily, and vice versa. Both have a sense of dynamic flow as their essence.

Remember the last moment when you felt supremely alive, most connected to the world. Were you giving birth, making love, standing at the top of a mountain, seeing an eclipse, riding a horse, playing a sport? Remember the feeling of energy moving through your trunk and limbs and out into space, into connection with others, into the world around you. What if these are developmental moments of lasting impact? The flow we feel at such moments is both effortless and deeply nutritive.

In embodied spirituality, we aspire to feel this flow, this developmental state, this quality of walking the spiritual path, more and more fully. We recognize how we shut it down with overly mental, conceptual control, too much top-down functioning, thinking that our innate way couldn't be the right way. When we recognize this developmental state and give it its due time and attention, this state is at once physical, relational, spiritual, and political. It is the fullest expression of our healing, creative selves.

In the next chapter, we'll examine the gateway that Buddhism and other spiritual traditions have used for millennia to help people access and revitalize their embodied spirituality: the breath.

7

THE BREATH OF LIFE

Learn how to exhale, the inhale will take care of itself.
—CARLA MELUCCI ARDITO

THE BREATH is a mysterious force, the basis of life in its own way. Before we are born, when we are still surrounded by fluid, we are breathing. As we live, our breath changes continuously, defying ideas about how it should come and go. The last breath of a dying person is momentous for those left behind.

The first step of embodiment is letting go of the breath. What does this mean? Most adults have become good at breathing in the way we think we should breathe—quietly and evenly.

For those of us who have practiced awareness of our breath—perhaps in meditation, yoga, exercise, or therapy—we may have trained ourselves to take a deep, abdominal breath whenever we notice our breath. The abdominal breath, or any breath in which we direct our breathing with intention, is what I call "cortical breathing." These are breaths directed from the cerebral cortex, top-down breaths. The alternative is "body-based breathing," initiated by the sum total of our activity and immediate metabolic needs. A body-based breath is initiated instinctively by the body and corresponds to what is needed physiologically, rather than what is habituated.

When we are in a state of breathing cortically, there is less body awareness and less continuity between sensation and breathing. The state is more mental, less physical. When we breathe with a cortical or intentional initiation, we generally pull or push the breath. Pulling in our inhalation and pushing out our exhalation adds a layer of effort to the breathing process, resulting in decreased efficiency. When we are anxious, we might add more control to the breathing process. Breathing in this way can actually increase our anxiety.

Body-Based Breathing

To move into body-based breathing, open your mouth wide and keep it open long enough and wide enough to feel a shift out of intentional, directed breathing. Wait for the breath to come on its own. Allow the next inhalation to come from your body without extra effort. Refrain from pulling the next inhalation in. Gently go past the thought, "Inhale now!" That is the cortical directive. Instead, *receive* the inhalation and *release* the exhalation. Let the breath come and go in its own rhythm.

After opening your mouth long enough and wide enough, you will feel the breath just come on its own, according to the metabolic conditions of the moment. There is a whole-body shift that occurs with this body-based breath. Wait for this shift, and feel it occur. Continue to rest quietly for a while. You will probably shift back to cortical breathing fairly quickly. When you notice you have done this, feel the difference. How does your overall state feel? Open your mouth again when you want to shift back into a body-based breath. Notice how that state feels. Over time you can come to know the difference between the two states quite deeply and become more habituated to body-based breathing.

Sadly, for many adults, jaw tension accompanies the cortical breath. If it is uncomfortable to open your mouth widely, place your hands on your cheeks and support your jaw gently as it opens as much as is comfortable. Slowly over time, your jaw will adjust to relaxing more as your breathing becomes more body based.

....

In Embodiment Practice, we want to keep shifting into body-based breathing. Unconscious habits are so powerful. We can make a shift into a new way of being and, thirty seconds later, find that we have unconsciously gone back to our habitual pattern. This is true of letting go of our breath, as well as any postural shift or emotional attitude. We just have to remember to let go of the breath over and over again. When I lead a session of Embodiment Practice, I might give that direction twenty times in an hour. This means that my students and I spend quite a bit of time with our mouths open. But only when we want to, when it feels right. If you find yourself getting too tight about letting go of the breath, picking at yourself too frequently, drop this focus until you want to come back to it. Only check in and notice your breath as much as you *want* to, especially at the beginning.

Yawning often accompanies the shift from a cortical breath to a noncortical one. Yawning allows a recalibration of the oxygen and carbon dioxide balance. Yawning is a release of the muscles involved in respiration, and it may or may not be due to fatigue. Yawning is rarely the sign of boredom that we have been taught it is.

In Embodiment Practice, whenever we feel like it, we can check our breath and see if it is free to come and go in whatever manner is most responsive to what is arising in our bodies in that moment. Body-based breathing feels looser, more open, and more relaxed. Practice letting go, opening your mouth, and learning to feel the shift from cortical breath to body-based breath. You can do this right now. Open your mouth and wait. Feel what happens in your body and with your breathing.

Often when we are anxious, we feel we cannot get a full breath. In response, we *pull in* our inhalation. The more we try to breathe deeply, the more obstructed our breath gets. If you open your mouth wide enough for long enough, the inhalation will come of its own accord. I promise. If you are afraid to try it, ask someone to sit with you while you do. The worst imaginable outcome is that you will pass out and then immediately inhale. This is what happens with children who hold their breath in anger. I have tried this with many, many people, and no one has ever passed out.

Mark, a professor of biological science, talked fast and grabbed snatches of breath on the run. On a good day, his anxiety was a low-level hum in the background. Now, as he struggled with a difficult divorce, anxiety was keeping him awake at night. He downloaded some meditation apps and went to the gym more frequently, but he was barely able to take the edge off his stress.

As we worked together on breathing, Mark understood the

idea of the cortical breath from a scientific point of view, and he could feel that he was pulling in his inhalation. As he began to work with letting go of the breath, he had to slow down his speech, feel his body as he spoke, and allow himself more time to breathe while talking. This was challenging. He felt his jaw tension more markedly. He became frustrated with his inability to make the shift easily. Within this process, he came to grips with the constant pressure of his own perfectionism. At one point, he cried with frustration. The whole difficult challenge of being human came crashing down on him. He was no longer able to evade his own limitations and mortality. As he emerged from crying, he started repeating quietly to himself, "This is the human condition. This is the human condition." He thought of all the shortcomings of the people around him and saw how he had let himself feel plagued by them, holding himself apart by a "higher" standard. As he saw this, his breath shifted. He sighed heavily. I said, "Mark, that was a released breath." "Oh yeah," he replied. "I'm tired." That night he was finally able to sleep.

VARIETIES OF BREATHING

Allowing even a single body-based breath can enliven any spiritual practice we engage in. When we practice such breathing, we are more able to feel the possibility of flowing with what is arising in our world. As we let go of controlling our breath, our belief in the necessity of top-down control seems to fade.

For the last few decades, the somatic world has emphasized abdominal breathing. Abdominal breathing means that the diaphragm moves fully downward into the abdominal cavity and the abdomen is pushed out with each inhalation. In many circles, abdominal breathing has come to be seen as full and correct breathing. It's true that abdominal breathing is often quite relaxing and can help shift us into a parasympathetic neurological state. (The autonomic nervous system is reflexive and unconscious. It sets the tone for all of our functioning as either sympathetic, attending to the external world, or parasympathetic, attending to the internal world.) These effects of abdominal breathing are true relative to its opposite—chest breathing. In this case, only the chest moves. It is a shallow breath. Chest breathing prepares us for aerobic action. It is both activated by and activates the sympathetic nervous system. It can increase our alertness and/or our anxiety, depending on how far we take it. Relative to chest breathing, abdominal breathing is often the better choice. However, from the perspective of body-based breathing, every possible type of breath is healthy at the right times, under the right circumstances. Of course, we always use both the chest and the abdomen to some degree when breathing.

Beyond the kind of abdominal and chest breathing already described, there are more subtle kinds of breathing. In meditation, we can also "settle" our breath, allowing it to become very calm and still. In yoga, we call this the "breath of no-breath." Both of these are related to what the Taoists call "embryonic breathing." In tai chi, it is taught that the breath should be long and thin. The length refers to the involvement of the whole core, from the top of the head to the pelvic floor. The thinness relates to being calm and settled. In Body-Mind Centering®, embryonic breathing is practiced in a way that requires a very calm, settled, parasympathetic state and enhanced fluid circulation.

Similarly, we have a cultural understanding of mouth breathing and nose breathing that sees mouth breathing as an expression of sympathetic neurological activation. When we are anxious, we often shift into this kind of breathing, which is on the continuum of panting. In contrast, nose breathing is more parasympathetic and healthier in general, because of the filtering mechanisms in our nostrils. However, consciously opening the mouth in a calm state is the beginning of a shift into a more balanced state of the autonomic nervous system and potentially a greater state of awareness. Our mouths are the first part of our neuromuscular systems to become functional, so that we can suck immediately after birth. In this way, our mouths become the foundation of our entire neuromuscular state. By relaxing the mouth, we relax our whole being.

Intentional opening of the mouth is a gateway to an intentional opening of our beings. We are not just letting go of the breath. We are potentially letting go of everything. As we let go of our fixed ideas about ourselves and the world, we open to what is. This is the perfect gateway into our next focus: the many details and levels of awareness involved in feeling the body.

8

Between Inside and Outside: The Portals, the Spine, and Core Flow

Mr. Duffy lived a short distance from his body.
—JAMES JOYCE, *DUBLINERS*

DESPITE THE BODY'S obvious primacy in life, reacquainting ourselves with it is, for most of us, like learning a new culture. Living as we do in the virtual reality of our mental realms, the body can seem like a foreign land. Once we have become so estranged, we mostly prefer it in short exposures. If the body is really hurt in one of the myriad ways that it can be—physically, emotionally, relationally, traumatically—then we often dedicate our lives to managing the exposure of those parts of ourselves, allowing some forms of embodiment but not others. This can hold true even for those of us who have years or decades of practice in a particular tradition, such as yoga or meditation. Such experience, though undoubtedly beneficial in its own right, is no guarantee that we have explored those aspects of our embodiment that are most troubling or frightening to us. Indeed, becoming "expert" in a given practice tradition can cause us to lose our beginner's mind and even lead to spiritual bypassing—using the forms and methods of the tradition to avoid looking squarely at the most tender or challenging patterns in our embodiment, behavior, and relationality.

I hope the previous chapters have given you fresh ways to begin to reconnect to your experience. If we gently and slowly refamiliarize ourselves with our sensations and bodies long enough and deeply enough, most of us move beyond our initial hesitation or habitual ways of practicing and hit a point at which we long to feel physically alive—the longing for embodiment.

So, without further ado, it is time to lay out some of the major themes and practices of this process. We'll begin doing so in this chapter and continue through Part Three, "Deepening and Blossoming." Some of this material might be a bit too detailed if you are in the early stages of gently immersing yourself in your body. Dip into these chapters as you like. Skip over whatever doesn't interest you for now. You can always come back to them. When you find details that seem too refined, just put them to the side, trusting that you can return to them when they feel relevant to your practice.

Deepening and Opening with the Breath

Our relationship with our breath can unfold to seemingly infinite potentials. On the most profound level, breath just happens. We don't do it. We don't own it. The world breathes, and these bodies are a part of that. Feel this possibility and let go of the breath if you like.

Physiologically, we have two levels of respiration. *External respiration* is the lungs' interface with air. On the cellular side of the process, we find *internal respiration*—the exchange of gases through the cell membrane. In order to understand this process more deeply, we first need to look at the fluid nature of the body.

The human body is mostly fluid, and the space within and

between cells is fluid. Intracellular fluid is within the cells, and interstitial fluid surrounds the cells. All bodily fluids comprise a unified whole. Just like the various oceans go by their own names but are all connected, the body has one system of fluid that circulates through the whole, passing through various membranes and thereby changing name and constituents—that is, what's in the fluid. Fluid circulation can be stagnant or turbulent. These variations can occur throughout the body or in pockets. In general, enhanced fluid circulation allows every cell increased access to fluid and the nutrients it circulates. Thus, enhanced fluid circulation allows us to breathe more fully.

This state of enhanced fluid circulation has a strong parasympathetic neurological component. The parasympathetic nervous system is the part of the nervous system that gears us to relax and absorb nourishment. As we go further into a relaxed and fluid state and our circulation is enhanced, our need for external respiration diminishes, and our breath can become very subtle, almost imperceptible. This goes toward the settled breath, the breath of no-breath, akin to the embryonic breathing we experience in utero. Underlying this fluid, relaxed inhalation is just the fact of opening on the inside, expanding the respiratory passage and the spaces around it. The whole mouth and nasal pharynx, including the soft palate and sinuses, have lots of capacity to open and expand, independent of big inhalations. Similarly, the entire chest can expand out in every direction, including downwardly. As the diaphragm becomes more and more alive and fully present, it shifts in ways that affect the pelvic organs and the fluid around them. As the diaphragm expands downward into the pelvis, all the pelvic organs can shift, and the whole pelvis and pelvic floor can follow suit, opening from the inside and expanding outward. Likewise, if the trunk expands in the directions of the shoulders and hips, this can begin a movement that can ripple out into the limbs, filling them with the energy of the breath, even though there is no respiratory cavity in the limbs.

This opening on the inside increases fluid circulation even further by literally pushing the fluids through the intercellular space from the inside out. Knowing and feeling this possibility of our breath opening from the inside can allow it to happen as part of the process of letting go of the breath without necessitating a large inhalation. This is a subtle possibility to explore gently within the larger context of letting go of the breath. Before discovering this subtler but more expansive route, I was so accustomed to preferring abdominal breathing that I would do that whenever I became aware of my breath.

Fluid Breath

Pause for a moment and see if you can contact a relatively relaxed state. Contemplate the fact that your body is mostly fluid, and see if your nervous system and muscles can relax into fluidity a bit more. Open your mouth without any expectation of inhaling, and allow whatever breath occurs. Remember a feeling of awe and wonder, what is known as having our breath taken away. Can you feel a subtle opening go through your whole body? Is there a feeling of having plenty of oxygen and only needing to breathe very gently? What else do you feel?

The Portals of the Body

Though the breath is often the first access point back into the body, it needs support from many different aspects of the self in order to find its fullest expression. I also like to teach about another facet of our embodiment, one that shapes our behavior and facilitates expressing our feelings and sensations in connection to the world. This is what I call the "portals" of the body. (Note to past readers and students: I used to call them "endpoints." New name, same idea.)

The portals of the body are the face/head, hands, feet, and pelvic floor. These are the places where the inner world and the outer world interact and exchange most obviously. On a physical level, our interactions with the world are transacted most directly by our faces and hands. However, the rest of our portals are just as sensitive and articulate. All the portals include "free ends" of the skeleton. For the face, that is the tip of the nose. The fingertips, the toes, and the tip of the coccyx or tailbone are the other free ends. The portals also contain the highest concentration of sensory nerve endings and a greater number of intrinsic, fine motor muscles than other body parts. For these reasons, the portals are the body parts most able to both give to and receive from the world. Our portals are the bridge between mindfulness of body, the first foundation of mindfulness, and mindfulness of phenomena (or outer world), the fourth foundation of mindfulness.

When we do Embodiment Practice, as our sensations begin to complete their physiological tasks, we might feel energy moving toward one of our portals. When the portal is awake enough to allow it, this energy can move out into the world in some way. Maybe there is a gesture of extending out. Maybe there is an actual exchange, taking an external object in. A sip of water? Passing the salt to a neighbor? Whatever the case, when our internal process moves through a portal and into the world, there is a feeling of completion that may be emotional or just energetic. Think of a feeling of happiness welling up inside you and becoming a smile. Or a sense of accomplishment filling your lower body and causing you to stand up taller. When we feel this sense of completion, we may have allowed an old emotion to move out or an old pattern to complete itself. For these reasons, during Embodiment Practice, we practice "waking up the portals." When we wake up the portals, we tell our sensations which way is out, where the door is.

Sensing Completion

Think of a dilemma or situation that you have resolved. Give your body lots of room to move and express. Think, "I'm done with that now." Perhaps think it repeatedly. See what your body does to affirm this. Perhaps there's a wave of relaxation. Does it reach any of the portals? Perhaps a gesture of completion arises. Keep giving permission and see what happens. Imagine what might happen if your body had full permission to express itself and safety to do so.

As our Embodiment Practice progresses, we may have a feeling of opening the portals to receive from the world. If our faces are scowling and our hands are fists, we will feel like we cannot get anything we want. We will feel cut off from the outside world. Waking up our portals allows us to shift into a more open, receptive place.

We wake up the portals the same way we do Embodiment Practice. We feel the sensations in the portals themselves and give them permission to move. Since sensory nerve endings are concentrated in the portals, there are lots of sensations to wake up.

FACE

As adults, we have practiced making our faces hide our feelings—"masking our faces." To do this, we numb out those sensations to a degree, but they can wake up relatively easily. As our faces open and soften, we can give and receive so much more readily, whether with other humans or with the world around us. Our faces become portals for love and authenticity rather than social masks.

Take a few moments to feel the sensations in your face and head, inside and out. Let your mouth soften and open if it likes. Give whatever you feel in your face and mouth permission to move, to breathe, to rest, to sound—whatever it wants to do, whatever is real.

Notice what emerges as you listen to your face. How does it change who you are? Does the softening in your face reach down into your throat or chest or belly? If your awareness shifts into the space around you, notice if the world has changed in any way.

Hands

Our hands are habitually in a role of servitude, constantly performing tasks for the whole self but rarely taking a moment for themselves. It takes a neurological shift to feel the sensations in our hands and let them do what *they* want to do. As with the face, however, this shift doesn't usually take a lot of time. As our hands wake up, we may experience more play, more ability to connect. The archetypal gesture of raising our hands to the sky is a powerful expression of embodied spirituality.

Feel the sensations in your hands, fingers, and wrists right now. Give your hands permission to move, breathe, rest, or sound however they like. Let them have a turn just to be for as long as they like. Let them wake up out of servitude into their own expressivity.

As your hands wake up, notice if the sensations move up your arms into your shoulders, maybe even into your chest and heart. Notice how these moments with your hands change you and, perhaps, the world around you.

Feet

Adult feet spend too much time imprisoned in shoes, which numbs their sensations. Feet need permission to touch and feel and also choose how much weight they want to bear. To let your feet have a turn, you may want to lie down. Make that choice by feeling your feet's preference.

As your feet wake up, they can offer you more support and a better connection to the ground, let alone to dance and play.

More awake feet can help the upper body to feel safer in the world and allow you to extend your awareness farther and farther out.

Feel the sensations in your feet, toes, and ankles. Give your feet permission to touch and push, move and breathe, scrunch up and spread out. If you get a cramp in your foot, let it stretch itself. Those are just muscles that are not used to moving. The more you move them, the less they will cramp.

As the sensations in your feet and toes increase, does that wake up your ankles and knees, legs and hips? What is different about you and your world when your legs and feet are more alive?

PELVIC FLOOR

The pelvic floor is the portal that can be a bit more complicated to reclaim. Often, the pelvic floor has been hidden away almost completely. Most of us don't know exactly what our pelvic floors are, and we have actively practiced not feeling sensations in them out of a fear of sexuality. The pelvic floor often takes more patience and kind attention to slowly wake up.

Between overly aggressive toilet training and the myriad pitfalls of human sexuality, the pelvic floor has often been chased into hiding. Many of us have an unconscious attitude that our pelvic floor is bad and dirty. Waking up the pelvic floor has to begin more gently and personally for most of us.

The pelvic floor is the base of the trunk. It has a muscular diaphragm composed of three muscles—the transversus perinei profundus, the levator ani, and the coccygeous). It is the job of these muscles to gently balance all movement of the trunk in the vertical plane—a big job, and one that goes well beyond elimination and sexuality! As you can see, the female and male pelvic floors are very similar.

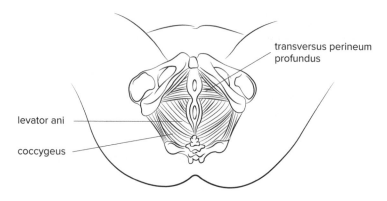

Female Pelvic floor

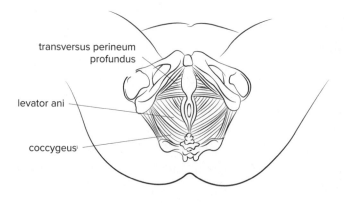

Male Pelvic floor

To begin reclaiming the pelvic
floor, I recommend getting to know
its anatomy more directly.
If you are comfortable doing so,
let the following exercise guide
you in tracing the skeletal
perimeter of your pelvic floor.

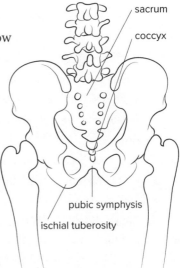

Take a wide stance and rub with both hands down the
back of your sacrum and tail.

The sacrum is bumpy and gently convex. The coccyx,
or tailbone, is two to four fused (or unfused, I like to
assert) pebble-like bones. If you have fallen on your coccyx, it is extremely painful and you are likely to remember. In this case, your coccyx may be bent and fused in
an extreme angle.

Look at the picture of the bones that form the perimeter of the pelvic floor. With your hands, explore the
space between your tail and your sitz bones (ischial
tuberosities). Trace the sitz bones around to the pubic
bone. They are one continuous bone on each side. Trace
the pubic symphysis (where the two pubic bones come
together) from top to bottom.

In any case, gingerly poke around a bit to get a sense

of what is happening there. Take a full, deep breath. That should sequence into the muscles of your pelvic floor, and you should feel a bit of movement in and around your tailbone. If you don't, squeeze your whole pelvic floor as tight as you can, then release the squeeze and take another breath. Can you feel any movement? Try coughing, sometimes that does it. Or close your mouth and bear down with your breath. Keep checking for the pelvic floor's ability to grasp up and in, then bulge down and out when it pushes. If you check in with your pelvic floor this way, over time it should regain its ability to participate in breathing.

Many of us are afraid to awaken the sensation and movement of the pelvic floor. Might it be a Pandora's box of sexuality? Often, however, people feel a deep calm, a sense of power and rootedness as the pelvic floor comes back to life. Furthermore, when the pelvic floor and the face can feel open at the same time, we have developed the capacity to start feeling the "core flow" through our bodies.

When you feel sufficiently familiar and comfortable with your pelvic floor, spend some time feeling its sensations and giving them the freedom to move, breathe, and sound just as you did with your other portals. It might take a bit more focus and relaxation, but try feeling your pelvic floor and letting go of your breath. What would your pelvic floor be doing right now if you were an animal or a child without any rules or inhibitions? What is the natural expression of what you're feeling in your pelvic floor right now? Come back again and again to the sensations, and let them live in their own way.

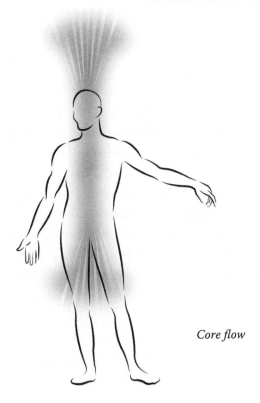

Core flow

CORE FLOW

As the pelvic floor wakes back up and is allowed to live freely along with the face, the flow between the two gets stronger and stronger. This core flow is the center of our aliveness and fundamental to embodied spiritual experience.

The core of the body includes the central nervous system, the skull and spine, the visceral organs, the endocrine glands, and potentially the whole trunk—muscles, fluids, and all. When people use the word *core* merely to refer to the muscles of the trunk, that is looking at the container. A more complex and holistic understanding comes from the Vedic traditions, which

describe the *sushumna*, the "central channel." While this is por-
trayed as a very thin channel of energy, other channels, or *nadis*,
flow around it.

My experience is that for most people, waking up an open
and generalized sense of flow through the core of the body
is a really important entry point for working with the tan-
tras, either Vedic or Buddhist, or even the Western sexually
focused versions.

First, we become comfortable waking up our portals,
including the pelvic floor. Then, as our portals wake up, the
pathways connecting them to each other awaken. As energy
can move more freely in and out of the portals, the core of the
body starts to wake up too. At this point, we can experience
periods of our attention/awareness being centered and rooted
in the core flow. Eventually, embodied awareness can rest in
our core flow *and* extend out to others, expanding and gathering in our attentional field but never becoming uprooted
or disembodied. This is what other mammals seem to do all
the time. We never see other mammals with their awareness
uprooted from their cores.

My Body-Mind Centering® teacher, Bonnie Bainbridge
Cohen, was once teaching a workshop in a very large room with
an industrial carpet, low ceilings, and no windows that could
open. There were several hundred people in the room. Bonnie
did not want the electromagnetic field of microphones near
her, and she could not be heard throughout the room speaking
with her normal voice with the mic so far away. She was totally
unperturbed. I saw her manifest a level of mastery that I had not
previously witnessed, something that I associate with dedicated
spiritual practice. Bonnie appeared to me to rest her awareness
unwaveringly and effortlessly in her core while simultaneously
holding the whole space, thousands of square feet and hundreds

Disembodied energy

of people, for a day and a half. When I described this to Bonnie, she attributed it to her somatic practices and said, "Thank you. I didn't know I was transmitting that."

Generally, most of our awareness is centered a bit in our foreheads and a bit in the space around us (as shown in the illustration opposite), not centered in the core as Bonnie demonstrated.

Core flow seems to be a hallmark of spiritual realization. As we get better at it and it gets stronger, our presence changes. Awakening and healing seem to occur more spontaneously. On the one hand, I have experienced very wise people who did not manifest a very strong core flow. Is it unnecessary to some people, or was it just not present as continuously? On the other hand, I have witnessed other teachers who are not focused on embodiment manifest this core flow. From this range of possibility, I surmise that a consciously embodied approach to spirituality is not required for core flow to be present. However, working toward core flow seems to help most of us move through obstacles and manifest the flow more fully. It all begins with waking up the portals, and it continues with articulating and lengthening the spine.

Our Miraculous Spines

Six joints between every vertebra! Clearly this structure is made for nearly constant movement. With the head on top and the pelvic floor at the bottom, there is a lot of awareness and interaction to initiate and guide all that potential spinal movement.

Sedentary lifestyles, modern furniture, and habitual emotional repression all conspire to inhibit spinal movement, congealing what should be a springy, bendy, twisty structure into something that feels sticky and achy. Most of us move our spines in large segments, with many of our vertebrae clumped together, unable to articulate independently.

Spinal movement and core flow are mutually connected and overlapping principles. Our spines are designed to sequence movement all the way up and all the way down, constantly and simultaneously. Potentially, several ripples of movement could move up and down the spine and pass through each other without congesting or conflicting.

Tracing the Back of the Spine

Sit on the edge of a chair and lean forward. You can also do this practice while lying down or standing. Try each at different times. Find the back of your pelvic floor and your tailbone (coccyx) with both hands, and lift your buttocks and anus up and out.

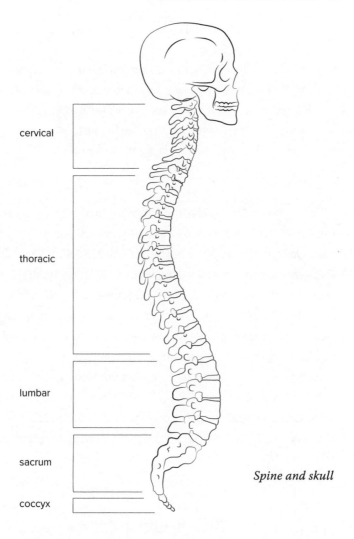

cervical

thoracic

lumbar

sacrum

coccyx

Spine and skull

Bring your fingertips together and trace up the center of your sacrum. Let your hands separate as they explore the edges of your sacrum. Touching your sacrum and spine in this way, move up your spine, exploring each vertebra as far up as you can go.

Let your hands jump up to the base of your skull and

explore downward as far as you can. If you can't reach your whole spine in this way, then try to contact the section of spine behind your heart by drawing your shoulder blades together toward your spine and then releasing them and letting them spread out to the side as far as they can go. Sense the vertebrae you were unable to touch. Maybe over time, it will get easier to reach them one by one.

The spine, including the spinal cord, can serve as a lightning rod between heaven and earth. Lots of energy and information comes into us through the portals of our head and pelvic floor. The spine, with its many joints, is made to move fluidly as this energy moves up and down the core. Over time, as you get to know your spine's habitual patterns, those patterns can start to loosen up. More and more movement can happen. Our spines can transform from rigid support systems to fluid lightning rods. Spines move in three fundamental ways, in two planes, and in three dimensions. They flex and extend forward and back in the sagittal plane, the plane of the wheel. They bend sideways, and they rotate, both in the vertical plane, the plane of the door.

Sagittal Undulation

Begin by either sitting or standing; each position has its advantages. Try one this time and the other another time. Rock your pelvis slowly and gently forward and back. Find a rhythm that allows the smoothest undulation from top to bottom. Notice which parts of your spine move fluidly. Let those parts slowly bring the other parts along. Which vertebrae feel like they move articulately and which feel clumped together in groups? Relax into the movement. Feel what shifts in your state of mind and body. Later, as you get good at this, try it lying down. The surface you lie on limits the movement, but that can help you clarify subtler articulation. Even if you have a spinal condition, such as arthritis or scoliosis, you can still do these practices. Just make sure you are being gentle and respectful of your limitations.

Undulating from Side to Side

This is the same as the last practice but in a different plane. Again, begin sitting, lying down, or standing, trying one this time and the others later. Rock your pelvis slowly and gently from side to side. Again, find a rhythm that allows the smoothest undulation from top to bottom. Notice which parts of your spine move more fluidly. Let those parts slowly bring the other parts along. Let any clumped vertebrae slowly let go of their fixed relationships. Relax into the movement. Feel what shifts in your state of mind and body.

Spinal Rotation

Again, begin either sitting or standing. Lying down is a bit more complicated, but do experiment with it at some point. Visualize, feel, and/or momentarily touch a spot near the tip of your tail/coccyx. If your tail is relaxed, it's just above and very slightly behind your anus. Begin to rotate your head to the right or left. Allow the rotation to continue down your spine into the small of your back. At this point, your rotation will probably have gotten more and more gradual until it moves into your pelvis. Resist the pelvic movement a bit and try to feel the rotation continue through your sacrum and the tip of your tail.

Then try the same rotation in the other direction.

Finally, rotate your head in one direction and let your pelvis counter the movement, like wringing out a rag. The bottom and the top move in opposite directions. (This can happen involuntarily if our spines are integrated. If it doesn't happen now or you can't tell, don't worry about it. Over a period of time, spinal awareness and movement can both increase.)

Try the counter-rotation with your head rotating in the other direction.

The spine and core flow are important in most approaches to embodied spirituality. As we focus on opening our hearts, lengthening our spines, and strengthening our core postural muscles, more and more energetic flow spontaneously occurs through our trunks. Even as I write this I am feeling more energy in my pelvis than I have ever previously accessed after sitting at a computer for hours.

As we open to greater energy flow through our cores, everything changes on every level. The simple phrases I've used to describe the first two steps in this book—"open your heart" and "feel your body"—can reveal previously unknown depth and nuance. Our conditioned selves can heal and release. Our true selves have more access to the unitive state. There are seemingly infinite possibilities unfolding in each of us uniquely, minutely, and gradually over time.

PART THREE

Deepening
and Blossoming

9

ENTERING THE STREAM OF EMBODIMENT PRACTICE

. . . .

IN THIS BOOK, we began with opening the heart. We explored the nature of our humanness and how we have become desynchronized with our bodies. We have begun to open the first gateway to deepening embodiment, letting go of the breath. And we have introduced ourselves to a number of aspects of feeling our bodies, including, importantly, our breath, spines, and portals. With this preparation, we are now ready to enter fully into Embodiment Practice—the formal practice that I have developed over several decades of teaching.

Although Embodiment Practice is the fruit of many years of practice and teaching, at its core it's very simple. In Embodiment Practice, we pause and feel the sensations in our bodies right now. Then comes the crux: we give those sensations permission to move, to breathe, to rest, to make sounds. We give them permission to express whatever and however they want. This is another way of phrasing step three on our path of embodied spirituality: allow what you discover in your heart and body to move you.

As we become more deeply acquainted with our bodies with their many and various parts, we feel more sensation from those parts. As we practice embodiment more, our attention span deepens and broadens to include more and more of ourselves for longer and longer. Eventually, our neurological baseline shifts out of the very desynchronized state predicated by modern human culture—feeling our bodies very superficially and infrequently—and deepens further and further into our own embodied birthright.

As you enter this territory, you may find an interesting dynamic emerging between feeling and allowing—steps two and three. It has a chicken-and-egg quality to it: feeling is a prerequisite for allowing, and allowing immediately deepens our sense of feeling, unfolding greater richness and detail in what we feel. This in turn affords new opportunities for acknowledging and allowing layers of our sensation and experience that we had not been in touch with before. And on and on. . . . Let's begin.

Embodiment Practice with a Sensation

Pick a particular sensation you notice in this moment. Take some time to really get to know it. What is its shape? Where is it located? Is it moving or still? As you attend to it, give it permission to do what it wants to do. If it moves through your body, that's fine. Let it. How does it want to breathe? Does it want to make a face, a sound, say any words? Is there an emotional tone there? What changes when you do all this? How does it feel? When you stop, pause and ask yourself why you stopped.

As you develop a deeper relationship to your body, you can ask questions of particular sensations: "What's going on with you? What do you want? What is happening?" As you get a feel for this sensation, you may want to ask more specific questions: "Are you sad? Are you angry about such and such?" When you are in contact with your body, you will feel a response to your communication, at the very least a yes or no—what the philosopher and psychologist Eugene Gendlin called a "felt shift." Do you want to try this now?

Asking Sensation

Let a particular sensation emerge in your attention. Let it do whatever it wants to do. Let it breathe in its own way. See if you have a question for this sensation. Continuing to feel the sensation and giving it permission to express itself, ask the question. See if you get a response, and if you feel moved to, ask a follow-up question. Continue for as long as you feel engaged by this dialogue.

Doing this now with myself, I felt a little collapse and constriction throughout my chest as I slouched slightly to type. I could blame the whole pattern on body mechanics and think I need to raise my computer a bit, but I am consistently raising and lowering it. I know there is more to this collapsed and constricted feeling in my chest right now. As I feel into the pattern, I can sense that my heart is at the center. Everything is collapsed and constricting around my heart. I ask myself and the pattern, "Why do you do this?" I get a complex of answers:

"It's easier. It's habitual. I can hide." I continue the conversation: "But it feels so good to be open and let my heart have room to be." The response: "Yes, it does." The next question: "Then why keep going back into the old pattern?" This does not get a real response, but I can feel the coziness of the habitual hiding. As I hold the question, it morphs: "How can I stay open?" The response: "Awareness." I feel a deep desire to remember again, to stay open, to be aware. On the one hand, there is a way that I want to hide. Writing is so exposing. I both want to hide and want to share and keep my heart open. I want to practice awareness more. This is a dialogue within my being. This is a moment of development.

Our portals can help us tremendously with this process. As our portals wake up to their own sensations, they naturally allow our movement out into the world around us. First we feel them, then we allow them to express themselves as subjective members of our internal community, not just as servants. As this new openness becomes integrated into our nervous systems and our behavior, the portals become a way of connecting to the world around us.

Sensations and the Portals

Rest into your body; feel your sensations; let go of your breath; and when you are ready, notice the particular sensations in your face and head right now. Give them permission to move, to breathe, to sound. Perhaps to speak. Feel any emotional tone that is there.

As your face wakes up, see if that moves your throat. Can your face reach down into your chest, your pelvis?

Can it connect to your pelvic floor? How has letting your face wake up changed the energy flow in your whole body?

Continue in the same way with each of the other portals—the hands, feet, and pelvic floor. As they become more integrated into your awareness, you can notice when a particular portal is not connecting to the world around you and give it more attention to help it wake up.

Instructions for Formal Embodiment Practice

The pith of this practice is to listen to sensations and give them permission to move and breathe, to rest, to sound, to do anything they like. In formal Embodiment Practice, we begin with letting go of our breath. We feel the sensations in our bodies and give them permission to express themselves. You now have all the tools to begin a formal individual embodiment session. You might want to pick a particular period of time, say fifteen minutes, so that if you drift away from your body, you can come back and make a little room for something to develop. If fifteen minutes feels too long, that's fine—go for five, if you can. This is all done in the spirit of kindness to yourself, dipping your toe in. Not rushing into the water if it feels cold, but slowly acclimating. You have the rest of your life to let this develop.

To review sequentially:

- Find a place that is comfortable, private, and safe.

- Feel your body and decide if you want to begin by lying down, sitting, or standing.

- ❧ Let go of your breath.

- ❧ Feel the sensations in your body right now.

- ❧ Let your attention go wherever it goes. Feel those sensations.

- ❧ Give those sensations permission to move, to breathe, to rest, to feel, to sound, to speak, however they want.

- ❧ Be kind enough to yourself to do exactly what feels right in this moment.

- ❧ Wake up your portals as you need to.

- ❧ Again and again, come from kindness.

- ❧ Continue, repeat, continue, repeat . . .

Often it can be helpful to take some time to write in a journal after doing Embodiment Practice. Notice if your writing feels different or if you discover new aspects of yourself.

If you do this practice a few days in a row, reflect on how that has affected you. Does anything feel different in your emotions, behavior, attitudes, heart, relationships, or work?

If you can do it every day for two weeks, you might notice more. Has your attention span during Embodiment Practice grown? Do you notice your body more throughout the day? Does this affect your ability to handle stress?

I hope you can find the optimal relationship to Embodiment Practice for yourself right now. It is very personal. Ideally, it is a gift to yourself. Sometimes we are not in the position to give it right away. That's okay. It will find its place in your psyche and emerge as and when appropriate.

Establishing the Rhythms of Practice

For many of us, finding a rhythm of practice is difficult. I had a wonderful young meditation student who was trying to meditate every day. She told me that the strangest thing was happening. She would sit down on her cushion in the morning and look at the clock and meditate, but when she would look back, "It was *still* the same minute!" She was going so deeply into her experience that time seemed to dissolve. I told her, "That's wonderful. Just keep sitting down and see what happens."

We judge ourselves. We think that some other approach is clearly better. That makes it really difficult to settle into what is right for us. This path of embodied spirituality requires tremendous creativity and deep listening. Perhaps brushing your teeth is an opportunity to practice mindfulness each day. Perhaps you forget for days at a time. Oh, well. Keep exploring.

With each practice, there is an optimum rhythm. Sabbath on Fridays. Church on Sundays. The call to prayers five times a day. If you can do something every day for two weeks, it can seep into your habitual nervous system. If you can do something every day for two months, it can establish roots. Once something has established roots, you can tailor it to your needs, and it will change over time.

Practice Journal

For some of us, tracking what practices we are doing each day can be very supportive. It offers a structure that allows us to explore this vast terrain of a personal path with more perseverance and dedication. Write down what you are doing each day, for how long, and what insights and experiences arise. Then reflect on it. Do you feel fully engaged in your path? Are you practicing enough? Are the practices you're currently doing exactly right for you right now? Does it all feel full and complete? Is there something further you are longing for? A dimension you could add that would feel nourishing? More solitude, more relationship? More embodiment, more reflection? More frequency, more depth? How can you let your path unfold as creatively as possible? Tracking your path as it develops over many years can be a deep way to witness yourself as you evolve.

In addition to tracking your practice life, taking time to write about your insights, experiences, and observations is an essential contemplative practice for many of us. Your practice journal can be a vehicle for that.

Throughout the rest of this book, we will be exploring further practices and aspects of the body. These can be practiced as independent meditations and can also be incorporated into your Embodiment Practice. As you explore them, notice the dance between feeling and allowing as it appears uniquely within you. Trust yourself. Do it your way. That's the only way it works.

10

CONNECTIONS, BOUNDARIES, AND THE FIVE FUNDAMENTAL ACTIONS

Emptiness contains fullness and fullness contains emptiness.
—CHÖGYAM TRUNGPA, *EVAM*

IN DAILY LIFE, when we feel stuck in some part of ourselves, waking up any one of the portals—face/head, hands, feet, or pelvic floor—may allow the energy to release. Life can flow unimpeded in one portal and out another. As this happens, the boundaries between our inner world and our outer world become both clearer and more permeable. Our portals and whole beings become more capable of negotiating with the world, receiving what we want and letting the rest flow past. We connect more easily to ourselves and others. Openness is an essential prerequisite to connectedness of every sort.

Paradoxically, as our inner experience becomes fuller, it is harder for noxious stimuli to invade us. Our fullness is, in itself, a protective boundary. We don't need to constrict ourselves or construct walls to keep safe.

Simultaneously, as the sensations in our portals, sensory organs, and skin wake up, we feel more vividly the continuity between ourselves and the world around us. Our awareness naturally sequences its focus from internal locations into the space around us, and vice versa. In fact, the more sensitively we relate to our internal space, the more we allow old conditioned structures to emerge and to be felt, healed, and released. Ironically, the more we ground into the physical body, the more our awareness naturally expands out into relationship with the world—physical, human, and spiritual. The downward direction of grounding supports an upward and outward expansion.

When this happens, our egotistical sense of duality can dissolve in a safe and psychologically healthy way. We no longer have the experience of being limited, isolated little selves. Our portals can help enormously with this. We can bring our embodied awareness into any physical or spiritual practice or any moment whatsoever.

Opening up and letting go into the world around us is related to emptiness, an essential concept and practice in Buddhism. Emptiness does not refer to emotional meaninglessness or hopelessness. It is intended to help us let go of our clinging to identity and instead feel continuity in the way I have just described it— the fluid interconnectedness of our inner and outer worlds. The Buddhist view is that we and everything around us are empty of being permanent, solid, independent objects. The Sanskrit word for "emptiness," *shunyata*, might also be translated as "boundlessness."

As we experience boundlessness, we do not become "boundaryless." Boundaries are an important concept in applied psychology, referring to clarity about relating with others. Knowing what we are feeling and what we want allows us to have clear boundaries with other people, to know when and how to connect and when and how to separate. Often when people have trouble with getting enmeshed with others, they try to strengthen their boundaries through some kind of fear-based

mental construct of separateness. While this may be a necessary and helpful stage, in embodied spirituality we aspire to go
beyond this kind of cognitive self-protectiveness. As the energy
radiating out from our cores becomes stronger and fuller, the
field around our bodies also becomes stronger and fuller, as
well as more coherent. Somehow, in a way we don't as yet have
a thorough scientific explanation for, this relates to our electromagnetic field. We experience a fullness that extends around
the whole body. This fullness is an effortless boundary that dis-
criminates at a very subtle level. It protects so much more effectively and intelligently than mental constructs do. This kind of
protection is born out of embodiment rather than as a reactive
need to protect ourselves.

THE FIVE FUNDAMENTAL ACTIONS

Another dimension of our bodily dialogue between the inner
world and the outer one occurs through a set of fundamental actions. These actions are basic to all creatures with central nervous systems and were first articulated as a system by
Bonnie Bainbridge Cohen in her landmark book *Sensing, Feeling, and Action: The Experiential Anatomy of Body-Mind Centering*. They form the building blocks of all movement. I call
them the "five fundamental actions": yield, push, reach, grasp,
and pull.[8] Becoming familiar and in tune with these actions can
help expand and clarify our somatic vocabulary, making the
expression of our sensations in Embodiment Practice all the
more articulate and meaningful.

YIELD

Of the five fundamental actions, yield is the most important
to embodied spirituality. This action is present not only in

vertebrates, but also in the earliest and simplest of life-forms, single-celled organisms. Yielding is utterly relaxed but full. Open and permeable yet completely present. Picture a bubble landing on your fingertip. Picture a jellyfish in the water. Picture a lioness lying on the ground, watching her cubs.

For humans, yielding is relaxing into gravity but also into the fullness of our own beings, so it is multidimensional. Yielding is not collapsing. No part of us becomes lifeless, dull, passive, or inert. In terms of embodied spirituality, yield is what allows us to not only relax into the moment but also relax into feeling our bodies, clearing out any old, tense patterns that obscure presence, and finally, resting into a unitive state.

Push

Push follows yield both developmentally and evolutionarily. Pushing can be initiated in any portal—face, hands, feet, or pelvic floor. The pushing portal moves out toward the world, meeting its force. The muscles on the pushing surface elongate to meet the world, but then the muscles moving from the portal into the body all shorten, slightly and sequentially, as they move up the limb into the core of the body. Push is the action that allows us to differentiate ourselves from our world. It strengthens our sense of self and internal fullness. Picture a wolf standing erect and alert as it looks over its territory. All of its portals are pushing out, almost as if each hair is bristling with life.

On any path of embodied spirituality, we need enough push to find a starting point, to be clear about finding our unique path, and to have the strength to show up and stay the course moment after moment. Beyond this, too much push can become its own obstacle. We can become too bound up in ourselves or our dogma to experience our connection to the world or to even move forward and embrace any level of change.

REACH

As we yield into the moment and then push into definition, we can reach out into the space around us. Reach is the third of the five fundamental actions. Reaching is more than just a position. It is a state of mind, an openness, a curiosity. The reaching portal extends into space not knowing what it will find. Picture an infant reaching out toward a bright light, trying to touch the light. This magical quality is the essence of reach. On any spiritual path, we need to feel this kind of openness and expansion in our bodies to go beyond what we already know.

Once we have yielded into the present moment, pushed enough to show up, reached out into the unknown, we might just rest in a state of wonder, meditation, prayer, or connection. Allowing all of our portals to be active in these ways allows us to have a full-bodied experience of the present moment. Chögyam Trungpa Rinpoche taught the practice of "aimless wandering." Here, I emphasize the inherently embodied aspect of this practice.

Aimless Wandering

Take some time to wake up the portals of your body. Feel a sense of yielding spread through your whole body—soft, open, alive. Push enough to come up to standing and to support this soft, yielding state. Allow yourself to wander, inside or outside, within this state of open awareness. Go as slowly as you need to in order to stay present as you move through the world. Notice when you shift out of the moment or a part of your body. Come back. Wake back up. Relax. Open . . . continue wandering.

When you are drawn to an object, a place, a creature, feel the reaching sensations in your body that draw you toward it. Feel the literal movements of reaching in your face, your feet, your hands, your pelvic floor that move you closer to the object of your interest. Once you have arrived in a position that feels right, let yourself pause and attune to the object or creature or place. Feel that you are giving and receiving. Listen, learn, enjoy. Stay as long as you like. Wander away when you are ready.

Aimless wandering is a wonderful way to blend embodiment and walking meditation, not to mention a way to just enjoy the world.

GRASP AND PULL

The fourth and fifth fundamental actions are more specific in their functions and therefore a bit more limited in their application to embodied spirituality. These actions are grasp and pull. Once we have yielded into the present moment, pushed enough to show up, and reached out into the unknown, we may just rest in a state of wonder, meditation, prayer, or connection, as in aimless wandering practice. Other times we need to take hold of what we experience and bring it into our beings and our lives. We might recognize that an experience has been missing, forgotten, or neglected in our lives. What do we need to grasp on to that experience and pull it into ourselves? On a literal physical level, see if there is an object nearby that embodies something you need to remember.

Just now, I paused in my writing, found a rock, picked it up (grasping), and brought it to my lower belly (pulling). Often we need to bring things to our front midlines to most deeply receive from them. As I hold the rock, I yield and open to receiving from it. I think about the earth and my need to ground more, to settle into the physical world and the moment. The energy deep in my womb space becomes more active. Thank you, rock! Thank you, earth! So often moving forward on our paths is literally elemental.

Integrating the Five Fundamental Actions into Your Embodiment Practice

The more you practice yielding, pushing, reaching, grasping, and pulling, the more permission you are giving them to arise in your life. This will, in turn, give you more opportunity to integrate them into your life and your relationships. Similarly, you will notice the feeling that one of them is a bit asleep or repressed. You can dedicate some Embodiment Practice time to each of them as needed.

I find that everyone living in a modern culture needs more yielding, and Embodiment Practice is grounded in yielding. We listen to sensation and give it permission to manifest. That's yielding. Yet we may need lots of conscious time to yield into ourselves, into our lives, into gravity, into the challenges and dilemmas we face.

For some of us, pushing is similarly repressed and needs inviting. Others overuse it. Learn about yourself. Find what you need. Reach, as a step, is variable and unique, and grasp and pull are even more so. Over time, as you engage these fundamental actions, you will learn about your relationship with each of them, and you can make time to give them room to grow and develop. Of course, as you do this, you are growing and developing yourself, which is a precious thing in this world.

11

OUR INTERNAL COMMUNITY:
THE TISSUES AND FLUIDS OF OUR BODIES

Our bodies move as our minds move. The qualities
of any movement are a manifestation of how mind
is expressing through the body at the moment.
—BONNIE BAINBRIDGE COHEN, *SENSING,
FEELING, AND ACTION*

THE ELEMENTS OF our universe live in our bodies
as the various tissues and fluids that comprise us. Just
as each of us has unique relationships to each element, so too
do we have both innate and conditioned affinities to different
tissues and fluids.

The *Satipatthana Sutra*, the quintessential meditation sutra
of Buddhism (discussed in chapter 6), encourages us to "examine and reflect very closely upon this body." Within this sutra,
there are pages of detailed lists of body parts, tissues, fluids,
and systems—from marrow to spleen—offered for reflection.
Most Buddhist scholars agree that the point of this reflection is
to cut attachment to the body. However, from the perspective
of embodied spirituality, attachment can be most effectively

dissolved by feeling, familiarizing, and allowing rather than rejecting or transcending.

If we contemplate each of our body systems, over time we can come to sense our tissues and fluids more directly, responding to them when they are out of balance, receiving from each its natural and unique wisdom. Each part of us can step forward when it is in need and also as its particular wisdom is required. When do we need to sense the stability of the bones, the fullness of the organs, the fluidity of the whole body? In this way, we can transform our internal diversity into a strong community accustomed to sharing leadership.

MUSCLES

Muscles are right under the skin. Their work of shortening and lengthening produces some of the loudest sensations in our physiology. It is easy to feel our muscles when they are exerting themselves or are sore afterward. From there, we can readily come to feel them even as they shorten and lengthen more subtly.

Some of us are naturally very muscular, spontaneously aware of our muscles and actively moving them. Sitting still may not be our first preference. Moving meditations work better when muscles need to move.

Pause and scan through your body's muscles. Feel for areas of tension. Give those areas special permission to move, to shorten and lengthen. How do you do this? See if you can increase the tension in the areas that feel tense. Then relax and let go as much as possible. Do you feel better? If so, you have released some muscle tension. See if these movements of shortening and lengthening your muscles naturally invite other muscles to ripple and wake up. Change your position slightly if that helps your muscular movement ripple through your whole body more easily, like a cat or a horse. Both animals are great muscular sequencers. See if you can get a sense that your whole muscular system, from the soles of your feet to your scalp, is awake and present. What qualities does this muscular awareness bring to your whole being?

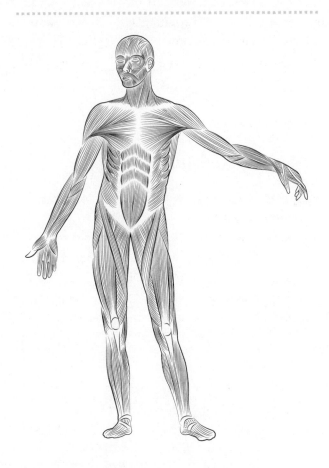

Skin and Nervous System

The skin and the nervous system function by sensing. Embryologically, they arise from the same tissue, and like the other sensory organs, the skin can be considered part of the nervous system. Some of us are especially sensitive in our skin and nervous systems, and that sensitivity is easily overstimulated and deregulated. Sitting or lying meditation can be a wonderful relief to overstimulated skin or nervous systems.

Our skin is easy to touch and sense, but we so often forget about it. Touch whatever part of your skin you can, even through your clothing. Let your touch tap into an awareness of the whole of your skin. As your skin wakes up, what changes in your state of being? Do you experience sensitivity, softness, permeability?

Skin Mindfulness Meditation

First ease your skin by touching it and by sensing its wholeness, from the soles of your feet to the top of your head. Give moments of awareness to the parts of your skin that aren't spontaneously included in your awareness of the whole. Meditate with the skin for a few moments or as long as you like. Afterward, notice what shifted in your state of mind as you felt your skin.

I wrote that the skin can be considered part of the nervous system, but what about the central and peripheral nervous systems that comprise it? What do they consist of? The brain fills the whole central cavity of the head. The spinal cord comes down from the center of the brain, out of the skull, and down the center of the spine. The peripheral nerves come out in pairs on each side of each vertebra.

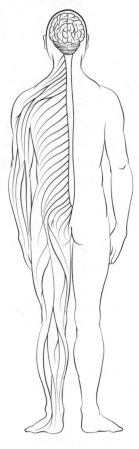

Nervous system

The nervous system is much more complicated to sense than the skin. The brain itself has no sensory nerve endings. So while it is sensing every other part of the body, it can't sense itself in the same direct manner. We can feel the nervous system less directly through fluid shifts and basic cellular aliveness, but this is subtler. Even more indirectly, we can sense the state of our nervous system by tracking our mental and sensory functioning. When we are agitated, we might speed up our speech and movement. Some people's nervous systems will spontaneously "power down" after prolonged overstimulation or fatigue.

My editor for this book, when reading this section, shared the following story. When his dog was a puppy, he took her to get groomed at a large corporate pet store. The dog, Kaya, a German shepherd mix, is extremely sensitive, and they treated her roughly for several hours. She was in an intense manic state when he picked her up—lunging and whining, and even giving off a strong smell of adrenalized fear. Once in the car, it was amazing to see how fast she powered down. Within ten seconds of lying down on the back seat, her nervous system had gone into a kind of trancelike sleep, in which she stayed for perhaps five or ten minutes. When she woke up, she was still a little skittish but quickly back to normal.

When the human nervous system is recovering from overstimulation, thinking and speech may become slow and labored. The eyelids may get droopy. Hearing may become a bit sketchy. By tracking your neurological function, over time you may become adept at neurological self-care, noticing when your nervous system is overworked.

We all think of our hearts as pulsating, and while the heart is the strongest pulsation in the body, everything else is pulsating too. The brain is the second strongest pulsator. Brain waves or oscillations are an aspect of brain pulsation, as are cranial sacral flow and a variety of other dynamics. The brain never stops pulsating until it is dead. Each brain center has its own pulsatory rhythm. Here's a good way to start getting in touch with this.

Brain as Jellyfish Visualization

Visualize your brain as a jellyfish. It is shaped a bit like a jellyfish, with the spinal cord and peripheral nerves as tendrils. Visualize your jellyfish brain undulating like jellyfish do. If you don't know what that looks like, find a video to watch before or during your meditation.

See how much you can relax into that visualization and actually feel some kind of physical undulation or release in your body. Let your breath and spine go with the visualization as much as they want to. Let this spread out your peripheral nerves into your whole body.

Afterward, take a few moments to notice what you got out of that meditation physically, mentally, psychologically, or spiritually. Check in with the sensations in your head. Can you assess your neurological function right now through your overall state, your vision, your thinking?

TONES OF THE NERVOUS SYSTEM—CONTROL, RELAXATION, INTENTION

Our nervous systems like to think of themselves as being in charge of life. This is a very short-term, small-minded reality. As Bonnie Bainbridge Cohen says, "The brain is the last to know." Our frontal lobes are designed to believe whatever they think, but they have far less control over our behavior than they would like to believe. In actuality, the lower brain centers, operating at a level below conscious control, are much more powerful in directing our behavior. One of my neuroscience teachers called his students who believed in free will "Free Willies." He saw all of our functioning as purely reflexive, mechanical, and material.

Letting our nervous systems relax and let go of the illusion of control is fundamental to any step forward on most spiritual paths. Our brains are not actually as in control as we like to think they are. When, however, they can open up and *listen* to the rest of the body as well, they are excellent consultants and facilitators. The jellyfish visualization can help with that. For many of us, our nervous systems are so tense that we can't even address the possibility of openness and relaxation, which is essential to becoming present and moving forward on our spiritual paths.

The other side of the coin of letting go is setting intention. Having a fluid, rhythmically pulsating nervous system allows us to set intention from a grounded, realistic, embodied place. When our nervous systems are too activated, intention is often overly ambitious or even totally unrelated to who we really are and where we are in our lives at the moment.

Trauma and Dissociation

A unique aspect of the nervous system is its ability to dramatically shut down when it is overwhelmed. Fight, flight, freeze, immobilize—we can activate to protect, defend, or move toward death in a complex variety of ways that affects our whole physiology. We call all of these ways "dissociation," and each type can become a powerful factor on our individual spiritual paths. Other mammals go into dissociative states when under threat and then shake them off once the physical threat is over. They can do this in a relatively quick and easy manner. It is more complicated for us humans.

Due to our unique frontal lobes, human dissociative states persist indefinitely, until we are able to consciously renegotiate our experience of being safe. Dissociative patterns interact with our developmental and spiritual paths in a variety of ways. They might draw us toward the spiritual as a contrast to the physical. Conversely, they might lead us to avoid the physical and the spiritual.

As we open to our experience on subtler and subtler levels, dissociative states and traumatic memories associated with them may emerge. This is common during spiritual practices. If there is no acknowledgment of this aspect of spiritual practice, then often practitioners feel alone and ashamed. As we open, we may find ourselves obsessed with memories or images. In our bodies, we may feel strong urges to fight or flee. Emotionally, we may be overwhelmed by fear, grief, or anger. On a subtler and ongoing level, we may have intense urges to avoid or distract. Practices that are designed to increase awareness naturally unearth dissociative patterns and lead practitioners to confusion and dilemmas regarding waking up and avoiding.

It is common for spiritual practitioners to remain stuck in this type of confusion until they recognize that this is actually a common aspect of the human experience. Once we acknowledge and understand this aspect of the spiritual path, then embodiment and relationship can provide a way to go beyond the initial paralysis and into a rich realm of personal development known as post-traumatic growth.

When you suspect that you are dissociating, you might want to seek professional help with that, learn more about it, tread gently, and find ways to move forward safely. Finding safe ways to move toward the present moment and your whole being allows awareness to spread through your body without

unconsciously having to avoid certain body parts or states. Ultimately, recognizing this particular psychophysical challenge of
being human leads us to have more compassion for ourselves
and all other beings.

The first step is for the nervous system to decide that it is
safe to be present. Then whatever body systems or parts were
most silenced can be slowly and gently invited back. This might
be like caring for a feral child or going into the backcountry to
let settlers know that a war is over. The muscles and movement
associated with the trauma often have to be repatterned. Fluid
circulation is often limited, and stagnancy needs to be cleared.
Visceral organs are often functioning at a minimal level and
need to be invited back.

VISCERA

Our visceral organs connect directly to our emotional brain
centers. How deeply we feel in our own hearts and bellies is
often reflected in our relationships to other people. Community, group, and relational practices can allow our organs and
emotional selves to clarify and develop. Conversely, developing more sensitivity to our organs can allow us to know ourselves better and feel that, even individually, each of our bodies
comprises a community of different feelings, resources, even
personalities. Finally, the organs are what bring the feeling of
fullness into our cores. This fullness is essential to being present
and authentic in any moment.

All of the organs of the body nestle together like a puppy
pile. There is hardly any fluid space around them. Each organ
pulsates in its own shape and rhythm, creating a polyrhythmic
symphony of nesting rhythms. In this way, the fullness of the
trunk is both very alive and very relaxed.

Organ Exploration/Meditation

This is a long one. Take it piece by piece, and let it go when you lose interest. Come back to it when you sense you want more.

Take a moment to locate your pelvic floor. If you are comfortable doing so, place your hand near or on it. The pelvic floor is the bottom of the trunk. Let it relax into your hand, whatever it might be touching, or the space around it.

As your pelvic floor relaxes, feel the organs directly above it relax down into it. The bladder, rectum, and genitals are directly connected to the pelvic floor.

As these lowest organs relax and rest on the pelvic floor, feel the next layer of organs relax down onto them. Remember the puppy pile. The bulk of what we think of as the belly is small intestine. Around the periphery of the small intestine is the large intestine. Behind the lower part of the intestines, some of us have the uterus and ovaries. Let all of these organs relax downward as well.

The next level of organs, around the waist area and starting in the back, comprises the kidneys, which rest half above and half below the lowest rib in the back. Place your hands in the kidney area and sense what is there. Give your kidneys permission to feel themselves again. With the adrenal glands resting like snow peaks on top of the kidneys, the latter are often overworked. Give them permission to breathe in their own way and eventually rest down on the support below.

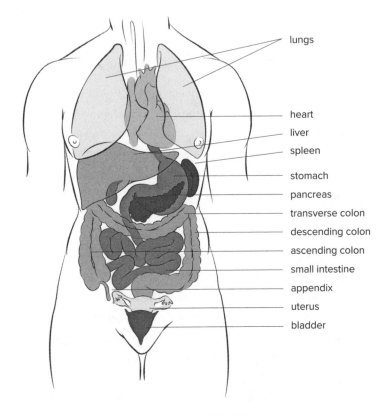

Visceral organs (MD SM 13)

Above the kidneys is the diaphragm. With your fingers, trace around the base of your rib cage. Your diaphragm attaches all the way around. It is not a visceral organ, but a muscle, dividing the chest from the abdomen. It is primarily active in breathing, knitting itself downward with inhalation and releasing upward with exhalation. (See picture of diaphragm underneath heart on p. 13.)

Filling most of the right side of the space below the diaphragm is the liver. The liver is a relatively flat organ, resting horizontally under the diaphragm, with the gall-bladder hanging under it just to the right of midline.

On the left side, the spleen is tucked under the dia-phragm. Just in front of that is the stomach. Underneath, in the center of the waist area and resting on the diago-nal, is the pancreas.

Take a gentle breath and feel/visually imagine all of these organs under the diaphragm. There is a lot going on in this part of the body. The different energies and functions of these organs can become chaotic and con-flicting, or they can harmonize and pulsate together in a restful manner. Pause and feel the internal sensa-tions below your diaphragm. As you inhale, feel your diaphragm press down gently on the organs below. As you exhale, feel all the organs gently shifting with the diaphragm as it moves up. Sense the fullness of all the organs from your pelvic floor to your diaphragm and how they rest together and harmonize their movement and pulsation.

Finally, the heart and lungs fill the chest. Their mem-branes, the pericardium of the heart and the pleura of the lungs, interdigitate with—grow into—the fascial membrane of the diaphragm. So when the diaphragm moves up and down, the membranes are pulled and pushed along with it. Furthermore, the lungs embrace the heart, leaving only a thin bit of heart uncovered in front (behind the sternum/breastbone) and in back (in front of the spine). Sense that your chest is filled by the heart and lungs and their containers. Sense how this fullness can rest down into the fullness below it.

The organs offer a lively fullness to our beings. Their involvement with our basic needs can bring an emotional authenticity to our spiritual practices.

The Endocrine System

The endocrine glands are located along the core of the body. Each of them are small bodies of tissue. We could hold all the endocrine tissue of the whole body in one hand. These small but potent energy centers generate hormones, which diffuse directly into the blood and out through the entire body in less than a minute. In this way, hormones create powerful and energetic states, changing moment to moment as each endocrine gland responds to the ever-changing blend of hormones circulating through the blood. In health, the endocrine glands work together in a balanced symphony. Our experience of this symphonic play of hormones is that of moving through various states of energy, from ecstasy to despair, arousal, bonding, anxiety, excitement, creative flow, athletic inspiration, ad infinitum. We could say that the endocrine system provides the depth and richness of our experience in the moment.

There are many systems of chakras, but all of them correspond directly to the endocrine system. In that sense any meditation that works with chakras is also working with that system. Endocrine imbalances come in many varieties. Parts of the system may be overworked. Other parts may be repressed and shut down. Meditating with the intention of regaining balance can address those habitual tendencies.

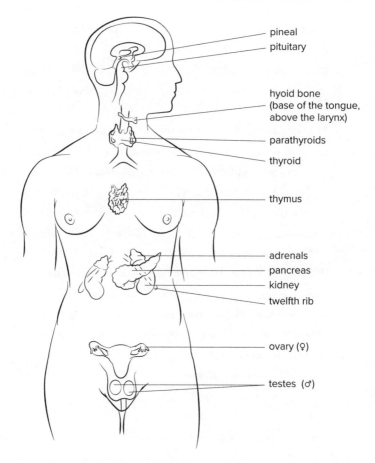

pineal
pituitary

hyoid bone
(base of the tongue,
above the larynx)

parathyroids

thyroid

thymus

adrenals
pancreas
kidney
twelfth rib

ovary (♀)

testes (♂)

Endocrine glands (MD SM 14)

Take a breath into the center of your pelvic floor, bringing your awareness to that center. Notice the feeling
there: energized, relaxed, tense, stagnant, whatever. Let
it articulate itself somehow, whatever comes to mind
verbally or visually.

Take a breath into the center of your pelvis. Sense

that center very widely at the place where the ovaries are located on each side in women. This is the same place from which the testes descend in men. In utero, both testes and ovaries were gonads there. Notice the feeling of that place.

Take a breath into the center of your waist area, sensing your pancreas right in the middle and your adrenals on top of your kidneys. Notice any feelings in this area.

Take a breath into the center of your chest and heart. Notice the state of this part of you. Is there a sense of openness, constriction? Any emotional tones there?

Take a breath into the center of your throat. How does this part feel? Is it able to let energy move through it?

Take a breath into the area right behind and between your eyebrows. Is there pressure? Relaxation? Openness?

Finally, breathe into the center of the top of your head. Is there an openness? Any agitation? Is there a sense of energy flowing in and out?

Over time you can become familiar with the sensations in each of these centers within your core. If you identify the endocrine glands involved, you may recognize the links between the physiological functions of those glands and the psychospiritual challenges you currently face.

FAT

In our culture of overabundance, fat is infamous. We are constantly fighting it and trying to get rid of it. In other cultures and times with leaner resources, fat was idealized. Fat is potentially balancing, nourishing, and protective when we allow it to be. I once dissected the body of a woman who seemed to be in her late sixties. When we took off her skin, she had the most beautiful fat, a golden layer that covered most of her. It was radiant. My projection was that she was a really cheerful, pleasant person, but there was enough fat that she might have been considered obese by our current medical standards.

> Touch your skin in a way that awakens it. Then touch it while feeling for the next layer underneath it. This is your fat. Light jiggling can allow you to touch the fat through the skin. No matter how skinny you are, there is always a thin layer of fat under your skin, between it and the muscle. Touch parts of your body that have more fat. If you have judgment about your fat, try to contemplate all of the positive qualities that fat brings—warmth, softness, insulation, energy, fluidity. Touch your fat with this in mind. Spend as long as you like, and see if you clear any of the negativity and awaken in its place a relaxed, full, fluid experience of fat. Know that you can come back to this again and again over time.

On a spiritual level, feeling comfortable with our fat can lend a fullness and physicality to relaxation, a sense of physical beingness.

Connective Tissue

The connective tissues are those that have fibers and fluid between the cells. Other kinds of tissue just have fluid between the cells. Connective tissues include fascia, muscles, tendons, ligaments, and bones. The fascia acts as a communication system and structural balancing system. A semifluid semi-membrane, the fascia lies just under the fat, sheathing all the muscles. The skeleton, with its rich and creative marrow in the long bones, grounds, structures, and creates a renewable source of strength and energy. This stable simplicity of the bones can be very calming and bring us back to the simple physical experience of now. Ligaments connect bone to bone, helping us to feel stable limits. Tendons connect muscle to bone, allowing us to transition between stability and movement.

On a spiritual level, our connective tissue lends us structure and stability to be present in this physical world, to stay grounded in physical reality. It reflects the balance and alignment between ourselves and the world. Much of embodied spirituality devotes itself to finding our center and aligning our connective tissues around that.

OUR FLUID BODIES

Our bodies are approximately 60 percent fluid, and at any given moment, 60 percent of that fluid is within our cells. Bodily fluid is constantly circulating. The cellular fluid passes through the cell membrane and becomes interstitial fluid, the fluid around and between cells. The interstitial fluid passes through a capillary wall and becomes blood, or it moves into a lymph vessel and becomes lymph. From the lymph or blood, the fluid can pass into a variety of local fluid depositories. Lymph may go to lymph vessels, the spleen, or an infection site. At the carotid artery, the lymph joins with the blood. Blood goes everywhere in the body, rejoins the interstitial fluid, and then moves inside the cells, bringing nutrients and becoming cellular fluid. The interstitial fluid in the kidneys becomes urine, and that in the brain becomes cerebrospinal fluid; the fluid in the eyes becomes tears, and that in the skin becomes sweat.

This constant circulation of fluids replicates the circulation of fluids on our planet; rain and snow becomes creeks, then rivers, and finally ocean. All of these evaporate into clouds, which precipitate again. Fluidity is a ubiquitous metaphor in psychological and spiritual philosophy: Go with the flow. Don't push the river. A rain of blessings. Thoughts are like waves, and resting mind is like the ocean depths.

In our bodies, when we are able to rest in the fluidity and flow of our actual physiology, we settle and calm. While fluidity and flow are not usually loud enough to be actual sensations, they are available to our awareness.

To become aware of fluidity and flow, we must first clear any loud or dominant phenomena, such as pain, strong sensation, intense emotion, and external stimuli that demand our attention. This may or may not be possible at any given moment. A hallmark of embodied spirituality is that we focus on sensations, emotions, or external situations that need our attention, rather than working stringently to free ourselves from those issues through mind control alone.

As we become comfortable enough with Embodiment Practice, we can allow strong sensations and emotions to move out of our bodies and be somewhat complete. At this point, we find ourselves in a state in which the sensations that arise are less distinct than pain or tension. These "global sensations" are relatively light and flowing. We may be able to sense a fluidity at that level.

By attending to our fluidity, we may be able to let our more rigid, overly focused ways of moving and being go. We may be able to rest in fluidity and flow. Just as we let go to float in water, we can let go into the energy of our natural fluidity. This is a powerful step toward allowing ourselves to be in this world, just as it is, just as we are.

Fluid Meditation

Feel your body. Think about the fact that it is predominantly fluid. Take a breath with the intention of letting go into that fluidity. Encourage all your tissues, especially your muscles, to let go and allow flow. Sense your nervous system being bathed in fluidity, releasing its stress and worry. Let your awareness of yourself as a fluid body permeate each part of you that comes to your awareness. When you are finished, notice what resources you have discovered.

There are infinite dimensions to the body and therefore infinite gateways to enter more deeply into its wisdom. Exploring the body systems gives us access to various qualities and allows us to experience a sense of internal community, with fluctuating degrees of connectedness and disjointedness, harmony and ignorance. May we all keep waking up to greater and greater awareness, not only *of* our bodies, but also *with* our bodies. The natural sensitivity and intelligence that arises from the body is essentially an animal awareness that has often been repressed, suppressed, dissociated from, or forgotten. Nevertheless, because it is our birthright, it comes back more quickly than most people imagine. All it takes is practice.

Integrating the resources of the body systems will happen organically, as you make time and space for them in your life and in your Embodiment Practice. Dedicate a bit of time to them as needed. Invite them into your meditations, your physical activities, and whatever practices are part of your routine. You are likely to find that the interweaving of feeling and allowing, steps two and three of embodied spirituality, grows ever more refined and interesting in this process. As you do, a gratifying depth and elemental richness will bloom in your life.

Part Four

The Path of Opening
and Connecting

12

THE MIND OF PRACTICE

Gradually, my heart, gradually everything happens
in its due course. The gardener could water a
hundred times, but fruit are not borne by force.

—KABIR

IN PARTS TWO and Three of this book, we explored a
wide range of information about the body and its systems, as well as many practices for beginning to sense ourselves
in layered, experiential ways. That information and related practices were grouped for coherence, but some of these practices
may have seemed too refined for you at this point in your self-
exploration. Perhaps you even feel a bit overwhelmed by all the
detail. If that's the case, don't worry—here in Part Four, we'll
back off the anatomical details in favor of integration, which is
simultaneously a process of deepening.

The key to such deepening is simple—it's practice. Practice is
our best path for reviewing, refining, and integrating what we've
learned, but not only that—it also opens us to making new and
spontaneous connections.

By now, you can feel the organic quality of the four steps of
embodied spirituality. We open our hearts and our minds to

newness, to what is fresh in this moment. This is step one—open. Step two is feel. We feel what is happening in our bodies—the sensations, the feelings, the emotions, the physiological shifts. As we integrate what we feel, we can safely allow—step three—the wildness of our bodies more and more room to express themselves. Finally, we come to step four, connecting. As we become more familiar with Embodiment Practice, releasing our habitual self-contraction in favor of feeling and allowing what wants to move in us and through us, we can explore more and more what it means for those expressions to connect to our surroundings and reverberate back to us. Sometimes this reciprocal process results in feeling challenged to open our hearts wider than they have been before. Thus, step four on the path of embodied spirituality—discovering the continuity between your heart, your body, and the world in its immediacy—reaches back and enfolds the previous three steps.

Through the repetition of practice, we find our way, and our opening can blossom into a much deeper connection with ourselves and with others—ultimately with the whole of nature, even the universe.

The mind of practice is the mind that wants to be nakedly present in this moment again and again. Although, for some beginners, this yearning for presence begins in a mental place, experience soon shows that true presence requires the body. A practice that comes exclusively from the mind and is imposed on the body bears no fruit. It is desire, arising from the heart, that refreshes our discipline and keeps our practice alive.

The mind of practice stands in stark contrast to the hungry mind, which is constantly looking for entertainment, pleasure, power, comfort, or somewhere to hide. The ground of embodied practice is to let the mind of practice take the lead, returning us to mindfulness of body and continually clarifying what we want. Sometimes those wants are ready to articulate in clear terms: "I want peace. I want simplicity. I want to have a clear and relaxed mind. I want to keep waking up. I want to have an open heart. I want to be present in my body. I want to dissolve into divine love and awareness." Commonly though, they need more time to incubate as bodily feelings or yearnings at the preverbal level.

The mind of practice realizes that what it wants is something that is already present and available if we just relax and use our mindfulness. The mind of practice recognizes how easily we get lost in worldly concerns—external phenomena—and how much effort is involved in returning from the hungry mind to the mind of this present moment.

First, we have to recognize, "Oh, I've gotten lost again." Then we have to slowly and gently lean back into the present moment—feel our bodies, even for one breath. This first breath, the baby step of returning to the moment, is harder than we think it should be. Often, we have to take that first breath many times in a row—many moments across many days—before we find our way to any kind of sustained presence.

Thinking it should come more easily than this, most people give up on themselves. I write this to encourage everyone. It *is* this difficult. And it's not just you. All we can do is keep remembering what we want and then, repeatedly and frequently, gently lean in.

Here's an example of the kind of gentle persistence I'm talking about. I have been writing this book for the better part of two decades. I have started it and re-envisioned it many times. Although there have been plenty of instances where I've thought I *should* be farther along, in truth, when I feel the most inspired to continue is when I begin once again with the heart.

How is it that the heart seems to lie quietly at the center of all our spiritual practices? Why is it that compassion practice seems to be the easy way to access all meditation practices and have the most long-term effect of any short-term meditation practice?[9] What is it about the heart, this numinous energy that is the center of our bodies and spirits simultaneously? I find it to be like the sun in the solar system, the essence of body and spirit.

With that in mind, let's revisit one of the simplest heart practices.

Heart Pulsation Meditation Revisited

Having begun to listen to your heart, perhaps you know which position you prefer at this point—sitting, standing, or lying down. Remember to try for a relaxed and symmetrical position in which your whole spine is resting at ease and as lengthened as possible. Perhaps you know how best to sense the pulsation of your heart. Is it with your hand on your heart in your chest, on the carotid artery in your neck, or on the radial artery in your wrist?

Wherever you begin, settle your attention and rest your mind in this sense of pulsation. Relax into the pulsation so that your whole body awareness can become this one pulse. Allow your mind to be absorbed in your heartbeat as fully as you like, for as long as you like.

Entering the Pulsatory World

The heart is the strongest generator of pulsation in the body, the brain is the second strongest, and everything else, all of the organs and cells, pulsate too. Not just that—we are always immersed in the pulsatory vibrations of other beings and external processes. Feeling the beat of our hearts is the gateway to entering the pulsatory world.

Reestablish or continue to sense the pulsatory quality of your heart. As you do, think of and sense all the other rhythms nestled around it. Every brain center, every visceral organ—all of them have a unique shape and rhythm. In health, these are all harmonious. Each muscle and even each bone pulsates. Every cell in the body pulsates. Right now and in every moment of your life, you are a symphony of pulsation.

Rest into the overall sense of pulsation. Relax your body into it so that your whole body awareness becomes pulsatory. If you can connect deeply enough to maintain it, take a slow, gentle walk in this rhythmic world. All of nature, the earth itself, even the universe, is pulsating, and that larger pulsation holds your own throbbing symphony with one rhythm nesting within each larger rhythm. Resting in pulsation is both blissful and elusive. How long can you allow yourself to live within this paradise?

As you open to the pulsation over time, you realize it is the essence of your body. It reverberates with all the pulsations around it. I was snorkeling in the Caribbean once. I submerged and found, for the first time, the glorious world of color and movement under the surface of the ocean. When I lifted my head out of the water, I was in the known world of sea and sky. When I resubmerged, there it was again—this magical reality coexisting next to the familiar, hidden without hiding.

The pulsatory world is like that as well. We have to let our heads "go under water"—that is, let go of the known, the labeled, the conceptually familiar. Pulsation is a natural transition into the unitive state. For most of us, it takes a period of opening to sensation, going under the waters of what feels culturally and personally familiar enough times that we become less insistent on conceptual reality. After that, the subtlety of pulsation becomes more accessible. Once you glimpse it, come back again and again to this state of pulsatory, unitive awareness. Rest there as long as you can.

The more we feel our hearts at this foundational and non-verbal level, the more we can begin to distinguish between the types of heart energy discussed in chapter 2: the egoic heart and the wise heart. When we can distinguish between the two, we can choose to open to our wise hearts. This is the next step in the heart meditation path and its natural outgrowth. Let's revisit a practice done earlier, again with new details.

Rediscovering the Wise Heart

Feel your body, your breath, and all the sensations that come to you. See if you can discern any emotional activity, sensations that seem emotional and unresolved. Can you sense the wise heart resting openly and peacefully around all those sensations? Ask the wiser, bigger heart if it can hold and soothe your confusion and emotional distress.

If it helps you to visualize, see one of these images in your mind's eye—a big heart cradling a smaller heart, a mother cradling a fussy child, a soothing color tempering a more tumultuous one.

As the sense of wisdom, peace, or joy spreads in your chest and the rest of your body, remember that this wise heart is always there; you just have to practice accessing it.

When you are ready to complete this practice, take a moment to see if there is anything specific to learn and remember from this time of meditation. What wisdom or truth is your heart offering you? Does it form into words or an image? Has your wise heart suggested any kind of allowing or acting within the circumstances of your life?

ALLOWING MINDFULNESS OF THE HEART TO EXPAND

Practicing with the heart draws us into the moment and into our bodily experiences, and this is a wonderful kind of mindfulness. Kindling mindfulness tends to happen most successfully when we have a clear focus, such as the heart's rhythm or the openness of the wise heart. At the same time, since the very nature of mindfulness is relational, it will naturally spread out to encompass more and more of our experience.

How do we invite this ever-expanding presence? We notice when we are lost in thoughts of the past and future. We notice when we leave this reality and enter fantasy. We practice coming back to this moment and this place.

As long as you have a body, it is the center of here and the center of now. Therefore, the essence of mindfulness is to listen to what is arising in your body right now. The first foundation of mindfulness is truly and unavoidably mindfulness of body.

If we listen to our sensations and allow their natural intelligence to emerge in our behavior, we find our way through life with greater ease and depth. We can feel when we are on our path, when we are awake, alive, and growing. As our bodily intelligence integrates with our cognition and our worldview, it becomes accessible. When we encounter a challenge, we naturally slow down, feeling our bodies and giving them permission to respond organically. This is in contrast to responding in a purely cognitive manner without taking into account our bodily and emotional experience. Without integrating our natural bodily intelligence, our responses to the world are a bit abstract. When we have practiced checking in with our bodies and our felt emotions, our natural intelligence can permeate all aspects of our lives, including our spirituality.

How do we do this? We need forms of practice, expression, ritual, and worship so we can join together, learn from each other, and deepen our presence and awareness. However, if we endeavor to share too intently, we begin to impose ourselves on others. In more extreme forms of imposition, such as the dogmas of organized religion, what should be encouragement for exploration tends to become rigid and moralistic. This one way becomes *the* way.

In the end, we each have to find what feels right and true

to us, and very often this is a matter of responding to what is already present rather than creating something new. By returning again and again to our own embodiment, our own natural human tendencies, we can discern the *feeling* of this moment, what is true now. That helps us find our own path.

Distinguishing Objects of Mindfulness

Sit quietly for a few moments until you feel present enough to discern what is arising in your field of awareness. Open to being mindful of your body. Notice the details of particular bodily sensations. Open to being mindful of your feelings. Let them untangle from your sensations. Is there any emotion or emotional tone present? Are you putting effort into this meditation? Do you feel yourself letting go?

Open to being mindful of your mind—thoughts, words, images, subtle thoughts involving some kind of attitude or effort, some shape of your attention. Can you be mindful of a general openness of mind, a mind that is resting and aware?

Open to being mindful of the phenomena outside you—sights, sounds, smells, tastes. How do all these focuses come together at the end of your practice? Are you shuttling from one to another? Do they unify into an overall state? What happens if you repeat this practice over time?

Expanding Mindfulness of the Body to New Activities

I hope the preceding practice helped you access an experience of "spontaneous mindfulness"—that is, mindfulness that doesn't rely on a predetermined object or focus but rather allows a focus to emerge from the field of awareness. Especially for beginners, this practice is challenging enough even while in a quiet room. Yet over time, it can expand to different contexts and activities.

Pick an activity that appeals to you, something you already do regularly or want to begin doing. This activity can become an opportunity to increase your awareness and give your body a bit more room to express itself. Perhaps the easiest option is sitting for a few minutes in nature or listening to music. For many people, walking serves as a gentle, accessible time to expand self-awareness. Moments of mindful embodiment practice can happen during running or exercise. Attend to the practice of running more subtly, monitoring speed, distance, bodily sensations, and subtle changes of gait. You can apply the same approach of increased awareness in dance or yoga. Any activity, even housework, can become more embodied. Growing your mindfulness of body and sensations in small, accessible increments is the foundation of embodiment. Perhaps you decide that, at each stoplight or in each cashier's line, you will check in with your body.

This kind of flexibility, which grows over time, can bear fruit in terms of our resilience in the unpredictability of day-to-day life. Increasingly, we can choose to bring the tools of embodied mindfulness to bear on situations as they arise.

Resolving Thoughts into Sensation

Take a moment to observe your body and its current state. Then choose a particular aspect of your life to think about. Intentionally let your thoughts explore it. Do this thoroughly enough that your body experiences the thought. When you are ready to step out of the thought, notice the sensations in your body. How are they different than the baseline you observed initially? Let your awareness rest in those sensations for as long as you like. Let the sensations dissolve back into some relatively neutral state. If you like, pick another situation in your life to contemplate. Try the whole meditation again.

13

Movement in Stillness: Embodied Meditation

Awareness is when movement and stillness become one.
—Dzogchen Ponlop Rinpoche

WHEN WE ARRIVE at a deep, meditative stillness, it is a gift, a form of grace. But we do not arrive there by holding still, by trying to meditate. We arrive by resting more and more deeply into the natural flow of life through our beings.

I have found exploring sensation and allowing its expression through movement to be transformative. That is why I teach Embodiment Practice—rather than solely sitting meditation— as the cornerstone of my approach to embodied spirituality. That said, sitting meditation offers us a window into our minds and is an important tool in many spiritual paths. We can arrive organically at stillness through Embodiment Practice simply by allowing stillness to emerge, or we can gently lean into it through embodied meditation.

In this chapter, we'll be exploring meditation through the lens of embodiment. The crux of this approach is to discover the interconnectedness and mutuality of movement and stillness.

Meditation means many things to many people, and indeed, there is an infinite number of ways to meditate. What does it mean to you? What do you want it to mean? Most people meditate by trying to pin their minds down. Picture a very slippery, scampering creature. We run around with outstretched hands trying to catch and contain our wild mind. When we catch it, we try to sit on it, pin it down, keep it still.

I recommend quite a different approach—the opposite, in many ways. I call this approach Embodied Meditation, and it is generally more enjoyable for most people. It is a huge relief for those who struggle with physical pain, and, as mentioned earlier, it moves us out of held, static stillness and offers access to dynamic stillness more readily.

In the *Satipatthana Sutra*, the Buddha says there are four ways to meditate: sitting, standing, lying, and walking. Each posture of meditation seems to be appropriate at different times and brings its own benefits. Though the possibilities of each way of meditating are infinite, they each have particular strengths. Sitting meditation is such a wonderful bridge between worldly life and spiritual life. Standing meditation can remind us of our strength and power. Lying meditation can bring ease and openness. Walking meditation brings our meditative state fully out into the world.

Beyond these four, there is also moving in other ways than walking. Embodiment Practice is a form of moving meditation. Dancing and yoga can be moving meditations. Whatever allows us to become more present and less absorbed in external reality and an objectified image of ourselves can be a form of meditation.

Posture and Meditation

When our beings are wrapped up in a particular struggle, when we try to be a certain way, or when difficult emotions arise and we resist them, our bodies take on the posture of this struggle. As we become aware of these postural distortions and find a way to be with whatever is coming up for us, our posture relaxes back into neutrality. This is perhaps the central dynamic of meditation—allowing what is already there and relaxing back in neutrality.

For most of us, relaxing into neutrality takes a bit of postural awareness. Some of the following details have been covered previously in this text, but because posture is so habitual, the details require a lot of repetition. Here are some of the keys:

- Parting the lips and teeth, thereby releasing the jaw and upper throat

- Allowing the whole face and head to move back and down, bringing the head back into alignment with the spine and trunk

- Lengthening the spine and feeling an ease of breath, movement, and energetic flow along your core, all the way up through the top of the head and down through the pelvic floor

- Rolling the shoulders back and down, letting the front of your chest open as much as the back

- Waking up the lower body and letting it participate fully

Adopting a neutral posture means that we are relaxed and our skeletons are aligned with gravity. To gently guide ourselves toward alignment, we balance the top and the bottom, the left and the right, and the front and the back.

Balance

Ah, the ephemeral possibility of balance! It sounds so right, and yet it is so elusive. Since life itself is constant change, we can approach balance, but we rarely achieve and even more rarely sustain it. Our bodies reflect that. Our posture is a moving approximation of being almost balanced. As we explore posture, even the balance of relaxation and effort is elusive. When we go too far with relaxing, we end up collapsing. When we go too far with effort, we end up tense.

There's reason that holding tension is referred to as being uptight. It's up, and it's tight—the very opposites of a relaxed relationship to gravity. Let's explore with a few brief practices.

Top and Bottom

Take a big breath as you pull yourself up and in. As you exhale, release the tension and the weight you were holding up and let yourself relax down. Release your face, your throat, your shoulders, your chest, and your diaphragm down into your belly. Let your belly, pelvis, legs, and feet soften down into the earth.

As we rest down into gravity, we release unnecessary tension and effort. This returns us to a more neutral open place that allows us to connect with the moment and the world around us more fully.

Balancing Left and Right

The two sides of the body are mostly symmetrical, with the exception of brain function and the visceral organs. There are so many balancing acts in our lives. Stillness and movement are the focus here, but there are lots of balance points—work and play, focus and openness, solitude and company, to name a few. As we move in and out of balance in our lives, we are naturally moving in and out of more and less symmetry in our bodies.

With the fingers of both hands, start at the tip of your chin and gently touch down along the midline of the front of your body. Notice as you do so how the sides feel the same or different. Let yourself become aware of any asymmetry, and encourage a release into balance as much as possible.

Hold both sides of your face with each hand. Again, feel for asymmetry and release whatever can let go easily.

Place both hands on the back of your skull and slowly move down the back midline as far as you are able. Go down as far as you can and then bring your arms around under your shoulders and begin as high up as you can, again moving slowly down the back, all the way to the tip of your coccyx. Once again, let your breath and your awareness release whatever you can, moving toward symmetry.

BALANCING FRONT AND BACK

The front and back of the body are so different. Our bellies are soft; other mammals keep this soft part to the ground most of the time. Our backs are mostly bone and muscle. Some systems correlate the front and the back with the future and the past. Each layer of the body touches and supports the layers around it. How can we explore and balance the relationship of front and back?

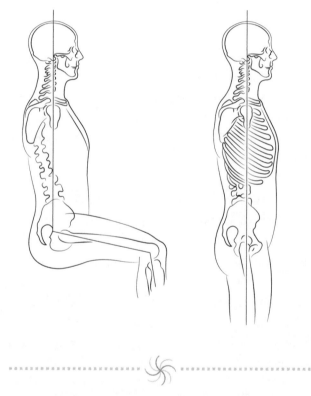

Place your hands on your face. Press back gently, bringing your face and head into alignment with your spine. Most people's faces and heads habitually reach forward. There is so much stimulation in our world; we overengage our senses and our brains, pulling ourselves off-center.

Put the fingertips of both hands on your sternum (breastbone). Lift your sternum straight up. Feel the breath fill the very top of your lungs, and release your shoulder blades and upper back. If you can, keep that open while you place both hands on the base of your rib cage in front and push the bottom of the rib cage back.

Put both hands on your hips. Wiggle your pelvis around and look for a place that feels like center.

In sitting meditation, the back can become stiff and uncomfortable. If this occurs, try breathing into your back—inflating, opening, and lengthening the back of your neck, lungs, kidneys, and pelvis. In this way, the back is supported by the breath. Try breathing into the "front of the back": the back of the throat, the back of the lungs, the front of the spine, and so on.

Another way of supporting the back is to let the front of the body hug the back of the body. Sometimes the reverse is helpful as well, hugging the front with the back. In either case, we highlight the middle and find a balanced relationship between front and back.

While finding the balance of front and back, imagine the centerline as it goes through your core, from the top of your head to the bottom of your pelvic floor. Does it feel continuous and flowing? Try visualizing and feeling the centerline as it passes through each part of you. Is it straight and continuous?

THE CENTERLINE

The centerline of the body is important in most spiritual traditions. The tree of life corresponds to the centerline in the Jewish Kabbalah tradition. In the Hindu tradition, we call the centerline the *sushumna*. In the Buddhist tradition, we call it the *avadhuti*. In the Catholic tradition, we make the sign of the cross along our front midline. I once heard a Native American teacher discussing the tradition of carving animal totems on tree trunks. He said, "Study the animals, but be like the tree."

The centerline correlates with the chakra system and the endocrine glands (see chapter 11). Each chakra is an energetic reflection of the endocrine glands in that area. Each chakra and each endocrine gland exist as part of the whole. Their health is reflected by the balance of the whole system. I encourage you to

study each chakra and each endocrine gland, but don't become fixated on any one in particular—stay true to your core flow.

The central flow of energy and awareness through the core of the body is the center of our awareness, the center of here and now. It connects us to heaven above us and to the earth below us. If our attention can rest, centered within that, then we may find our way to dynamic stillness. This is a path of deepening spirituality by going through the body versus controlling or transcending it.

EMBODIED MEDITATION

Let's try a session of Embodied Meditation now. You can integrate this into any open meditation practice you already do, or you can just try it on its own. In terms of the four steps of embodied spirituality, first, *open* to the idea of including your body in meditation. Second, *feel* your body as you meditate. Don't repress what is happening inside you. Third, *allow* your bodily experience permission to move, to breathe freely, in its own way. Ultimately, this is self-compassion, kindness to yourself. Fourth, open again and in that opening, feel the connection that happens naturally, the connection that, in fact, already exists. *Connect* to yourself, your body, your breath, in this moment amid the whole big and beautiful world around you.

To begin, settle down and go through any or all of the three awareness and movement exercises already covered in this chapter—balancing top and bottom, left and right, front and back. As you settle more, become aware of your current state of body—sensations and the gentle movement of your breath. Become aware of your current state of mind—thoughts, perceptions, feeling tone. At that point you are here, now, being with what is.

If your mind is running around in circles, so be it. Minds run around in circles sometimes. Be with that.

If your heart is broken and you think, "I can't stand this," just be kind and do your best. You can probably stand more than you think you can. Just this moment, be with it. Let it breathe. Notice if you feel a tad better. Appreciate that. Repeat as many times as you want. Then take a break. Come back later when you feel like it.

Whatever is happening in this present moment, gently embrace it with awareness. Let go and relax. You can do it while you read, if you read slowly and pause between sentences. Release any extra tension in your body. Find the center of your body and let everything unwind around that. Perhaps your shoulders are pulling forward and up; release them. Perhaps your face is reaching forward; let your whole head rest back. As you become aware of any part of your body that is not resting into your center and down into the earth, let it go.

This is a subtle process that occurs over time. To continue to stay here and now, feel your whole body gently shift with each inhalation and exhalation.

At a certain point, as your body unwinds, you may become aware that your mind is holding on. Right at this moment inevitably and inexorably, your mind is holding on to being you. Being a particular kind of person in this particular moment. Take a deep breath, and as you let it go, let go of trying to meditate. Another breath—let go of trying to be better. Another—what else can you let go of?

On a subtle level, we squeeze parts of ourselves, trying to be focused or still or even just to be ourselves.

Take a breath and let the energy of your head go. Imagine the energy is light, and let the light spread out into the space around your head. With the next breath, release your heart in the same way. Here it is, let your heart shine like the sun. Warm and bright and continuous. Another breath—release the energy of your belly and pelvis gently and evenly in all directions.

This is energetic freedom. This is meditation.

Generally, when we hear a sound, the mind is captured by that sound. What is it? We automatically focus on identifying the sound. Same thing with sights. Close your eyes, turn your head, and look. See if you can perceive your mind scrambling to identify each form in its visual field. Once you have categorized all the sights and sounds, a part of your mind is busy monitoring and maintaining this worldview. Can you perceive that?

Instead, relax your eyes and ears. See and hear without identifying.

This is freedom. Freedom is pleasurable. Meditation is pleasurable. Let go and relax.

When there is pain that needs to be attended to, the sooner you attend to it, the sooner it can release. Attending to pain feels good after a while, with a bit of practice. It is a normal part of meditation. Soften toward the pain. Hold it, love it, soothe it. Let it shift if it wants to. Feel your breath.

This is Embodied Meditation.

14

ELEMENTS OF PRESENCE

Once you have had a glimpse of awarness or Presence, you
know it firsthand. . . . You can invite Presence into your life.
—ECKHART TOLLE, *A NEW EARTH*

ONCE WE IMMERSE OURSELVES in Embodiment
Practice and Embodied Meditation, we begin to live
more and more in the present moment. The present moment
opens us up to the space around us, and we realize we are part
of the world. We experience the unitive state, a sense of oneness
with our environment, a sense of presence. We do not lose our
individuality as is implied in the dissolution model—we gain
our universality. The drop does not dissolve in the ocean; the
ocean awakens in the drop.[10]

A student of mine, Avani, is going through treatment for
a difficult cancer. She is very mature in her embodiment and
teaches it throughout the world. On the one hand, she looks
emaciated and suddenly appears "old." She has lost so much—
several body parts, her work. On the other hand, she laughs,
dances, sings, and enjoys nature. Her doctors are in awe of her
ability to be so present with such a challenging process. She

feels held by love. Her presence is very loving; the "presence" of love surrounds her.

This is the experiential territory encompassed by the phrase "embodied spirituality." It's not a matter of belief or adherence to any particular philosophy but rather a powerful feeling of aliveness in this moment.

Cellular Consciousness

The mind is in every cell of the body.
—Candace Pert, *Molecules of Emotion*

Show me any definition of consciousness in the textbook, and I'll show you a protist [single-celled organism] that can fit it.
—Lynn Margulis, *Microcosmos*

We can shift from experiencing our bodies as a collection of sensations to feeling them as an energy field. As we practice sensory awareness, our attention grows, both in breadth and in depth. We become more and more sensitive to subtler and subtler levels of sensation. Finally, we go beyond sensation at the level detected by our sensory nerves and are able to sense pulsation, which is detected indirectly as it produces miniscule movements in the tissues that are monitored by the nervous system. In this way, we can become aware at deeper levels of the body—eventually all the way down to our cells. Cellular consciousness is an important link between sensation and pulsation, awareness and presence.

Bruce Lipton, a cellular biologist, tells us that cells can be in two different modes of functioning: growth or protection. "The human blood vessel cells I studied at Stanford exhibited one microscopic anatomy for providing nutrition and a completely different microscopic anatomy for providing a protection response," he writes. "What they couldn't do was exhibit both configurations at the same time."[11]

There are about 37 trillion human cells in each of our bodies. How many of your cells are in growth mode right now, and how many are in protection mode? We don't currently have a method to measure this, but we can hypothesize.

Purely speculatively, in extreme situations rapidly approaching death, we might have less than 50 percent in growth mode. As we move closer and closer to death, this percentage would decline to zero. In the normal waking state of a habitually body-avoidant person, probably less than 65 percent are in growth mode. In my most awake experiences for extended periods of time, do I get up to 85 percent? Who knows? Even imagining our cells' states of consciousness feels awakening. We can use this yardstick of our cells' functioning to get a sense of our embodiment. Though it is only hypothetical, it helps us move away from a reductionistic measure of embodiment. Embodiment is too complex to simply be a matter of being *in* or *out* of our bodies. Cell consciousness brings dimensionality—a depth and breadth—to our experience of embodiment.

Touching Cellular Consciousness

Wherever you are, whatever you're doing, pause for a moment. Think, imagine, feel that you are a conglomeration of 37 trillion human cells and 370 trillion bacterial cells.[12] These bacteria are mostly in your intestines, helping you digest. All that life! Each cell is burgeoning with life activity, millions of chemical creations and dissolutions in each second. What do you feel when you bring your awareness to your cells? What happens when you mentally free your cells to create, to do whatever they want to do right now? Notice areas of your body that feel more alive, and let that aliveness spread into any areas that feel more numb or dissociated.

Cellular consciousness develops with time and attention. First, begin just touching the idea of your cells in this way. Let this grow into an awareness *of* your cells. See how that evolves into more sensation and energy as it moves toward cellular consciousness.

In *The Mind of the Cells*, Satprem recounts some of his experiences with his teacher, Mira Alfassa, who was known to her students as "the Mother." As the Mother approached her death, she shared the shift from mental and bodily consciousness into cellular consciousness. She felt that the cells were able to hold a much more powerful and vast consciousness that was divine and immortal. She shared, "Whenever I ask my body what *it* wants, all the cells reply, 'We are immortal, we want to be immortal.'"

If this sounds too magical for you, consider the following quote from Alexis Carrel, a twentieth-century Nobel laureate in physiology: "The cell is immortal. It is merely the fluid in which it floats that degenerates. Renew the fluid at intervals, give the cells what they require for nutrition and, as far as we know, the pulsation of life may go on forever."[13] As an example, consider the cells of Henrietta Lacks, an African American woman whose cancer cells were cultured in 1951, the year she died, and have remained alive in cell lines throughout the ensuing seventy years, with no end in sight.[14]

Perhaps this is a clue that cellular awareness (our awareness of our cells) and cellular consciousness (the mind of the cells) is an important link between embodiment and spirituality. Bonnie Bainbridge Cohen, the creator of Body-Mind Centering®, says, "The process of embodiment is a being process, not a doing process, not a thinking process. It is an awareness process in which the guide and witness dissolve into cellular consciousness."[15]

Remembering that our cells exist can be the entrance to this experience. As we become accustomed to remembering our cells, we begin to experience them. It is not so much a matter of feeling new sensations as a subtle shift in perception. It is a matter of entering rather than observing from the outside. It is the intersection between the pulsation of our physiology, the fluidity of our bodies, and a sense of wholeness, but not so much of self. It is an experience we rest into over time. Our cells are available to us every moment of every day. Whenever you need help, shift your awareness toward your cells, as in the earlier meditation, even for a few moments. Not only can it connect you to a nearly inexhaustible resource, it can lead you to previously unimagined solutions. Try it again now if you like.

As your path of embodied spirituality evolves, cellular consciousness may come to play a larger part. Any aspect of embodiment can include the dimension of cellular consciousness. The possibility of long-term, dedicated embodiment practice is that every cell in the body can awaken into sensation and awareness.

MINDFULNESS OF NATURE

As our mindfulness of body deepens, it naturally blossoms into a mindfulness of phenomena, as it did for me when I yielded to the rock (described in chapter 10). I pause as I type this now and rest into my body. I feel a weariness that pervades me—too much time on the computer. As I yield into the weariness, I also yield into gravity. I feel the weight of my body through my sitbones and into the chair. I immediately glance out the window—seeking without thought the sky and trees. Ah, relief and nourishment!

Nature is full of phenomena that can teach and enrich us. Our physical world—this beautiful planet, with its miraculously life-giving sun and atmosphere—forms a biosphere, a living womb that supports all living creatures. Our biosphere not only nourishes us, it draws us out of our small-minded egotism. It teaches us about interconnection and interbeing. We are all unified within the biosphere. Don Miguel Ruiz teaches that humanity is an organ within the body of the world.[16] Brian Swimme, a mathematician and evolutionary cosmologist, teaches that humans are the self-aware function of the universe and that our purpose is to gawk at the wonders of its beauty and splendor.[17] Reflecting on these teachings brings me a sense of belonging and humility simultaneously.

As our embodiment blossoms into connection with the larger world, nature can heal us and teach us more and more actively. As we come to know ourselves as a part of this living world, embodied spirituality often blossoms into a desire to serve the world, to protect the earth, humanity, and all other life-forms within it. We are truly part of this living planet, our biosphere. We are part of the stream of life that has been living on the earth for almost four billion years. We are part of the living body of the earth and the whole universe for that matter. As we feel our bodies and allow them to complete with their emotional patterns, we clear the way to feel in our bodies the continuity between our own life force and the movement of the universe. The unitive state becomes a deeply felt reality of connectedness. In this way, spirituality can evolve into environmental and social activism. If activism is grounded in embodiment, then we move forward with compassion for ourselves and others. This circumvents our tendencies to polarize in relationship to those who have experiences different than our own. Rather than seeing such people as threatening, we can look at them with the invigorating sense, "Another expression of mindfulness of phenomena!" We can recognize that we are all truly in this together.

Umbilical Earth Meditation

Whenever you can, renew your connection to the earth by lying on it. Place your belly on the earth and feel the connection, like an umbilical cord from your belly button into the earth. The earth is the mother that has always supported us. She readily receives our full weight, holding us, providing us with everything we need to live.

Feeling this, let your body relax, open, and connect to the earth and the biosphere around you. The earth, like every living body, has a pulsatory electromagnetic field. Let your own pulsatory rhythms and your whole self be bathed in the energy of the earth.

WATER

Once, in British Columbia, I hiked down to an inland waterway. It was a crossroads of four different bodies of water, each surrounded by mountains covered with evergreens. It was a clear, sunny day, warm enough that I could ease into the water and float on my back right at the center of it all. From that vantage point, there was no evidence of human existence in sight.

All the elements converged around my naked, meditating little body. My mind let go fairly completely, and there was an experience of balance and continuity. The earth, water, air, and light of my body continuously pulsated with the pulsations of the earth, water, air, and sunlight around me.

Whenever I enter a body of natural water, I sense the continuity of all the waters of the earth—especially the oceans. This is so rejuvenating physically and emotionally, and simultaneously, it takes me out of my little self and into the great being of this world.

Sensing this continuity of life through water isn't just a matter of external bodies of water—it's also something we carry with us all the time. All our bodily fluids have the same foundational constituents as seawater. Earliest life was just a membrane around seawater. As we evolved, the inner ocean continued. No matter how far we are from the water, we carry it with us, inside us. Feeling our internal, predominant fluidity is a constant opportunity to enter a world that is soft and nourishing, an ever-replenishing fountain of vitality. Feel it now.

AIR

In most traditions, the earth is the elemental mother. This is the view in Chinese medicine as well, but here the air is added as the father element. In the same way that the earth has never shirked away from holding us, the air comes right up to and into us.

Our breath is the center of our living experience. Any practice can become more potent when the breath is integrated into it. The air offers itself to us as nourishment, as cleansing, and as support. It inspires us with its freshness and vastness. Air and space are mutual aspects of the same elemental wisdom. When we look at the sky, we see both the air and then outer space beyond it. This offers us a reminder of how vast the world is and how small and momentary we are. Vastness inspires us to let go, and let go, and let go further.

LIGHT

How is light a part of embodied spirituality? Obviously, we need the warmth of the sun to sustain life. Sunlight lifts our spirits and encourages us to expand. But again, to think of light only as external to us is only a partial view. We *contain* light. Photons are packets of electromagnetic energy. They enter our eyes when we see light. They enter our bodies via radiation. And our bodies generate photons, producing bioluminescence. We glow! Generally this occurs at a level way below our ability to perceive it. In all these ways, light is part of our physicality.

Beyond this, the seasons, with their changes in light, affect us profoundly. Moonlight pulls on our internal tides just as it does on the ocean. This is evidenced in hormonal rhythms as well as growth patterns in all plant and animal species. Though we have found no scientific evidence that starlight changes us, surely it must. What does it mean to have photons from millions of light years away enter our eyes?

The sun gods and goddesses are too numerous to name—Atum, Shamash, Inti, Helios, Apollo, Awondo, Tonatiuh, Shams, Suryaprabha, Saulé, Áine. Of all the elements, light seems the most elevated yet also the most elusive. We depict light emanating in orbs around our saints' energy centers. We talk of "seeing the light," "the light body," "going toward the light," "the rainbow body." In all of these expressions, light is fundamentally linked to some kind of liberation.

Our sense organs connect us to the external world, yet everything they perceive is filtered through our nervous system and its expectations. As verbal, thinking animals, our sense perceptions are ruled by concepts. Our perceptions are heavily mediated by what we believe to be true. We perceive what we expect to perceive.

Among all our sense organs, our eyes are perhaps most dominated by our nervous systems. Allan Schore described the eye as the visible portion of the nervous system.[18] When we look directly at light, we move beyond conceptual vision, the habit of seeing labels and entities. We move more fully into the moment. This is a powerful practice. If you try it, practice embodiment first. Otherwise, you might become ungrounded and disoriented.

Find a place to sit, stand, or lie down where your eyes can rest on a simple image, perhaps looking at a wall, at the ceiling, or into a cloudless sky. Begin as always by resting comfortably into your body and releasing control over your breath. When you are ready, let your eyes relax. Let the image in front of you enter your being rather than reaching out toward it with your eyes. Notice the labeling part of your mind and encourage it to relax. Work toward letting go of identifying what you see. Let the light pour into your eyes. Relax with that, open to that. Feel how it affects your whole being.

As we work with perceiving external light more directly, our bodies become lighter in their sensations. We feel as if we are filled with light. As the feeling of lightness penetrates all the way to our core, it spills back out. We feel radiant. In working with this, a mantra spontaneously arose for me: "See the light, feel the light, be the light."

Five Female Buddhas

In Indian and Tibetan Buddhism, each of the elements is regarded as one of the five female buddhas. Space is the buddha Dhatvishvari. The earth is Buddhalocana. Water is the buddha Mamaki. Fire is the buddha Pandaravasini. The wind is the buddha Samayatara, or Green Tara.

This characterization acknowledges the sacred, mothering aspect of the elements. It reminds us to receive from the elements, to take their presence and healing energy into our bodies. Perhaps we are moved to make offerings to the elements through words or movement or actual substances—flowers, water, food. By offering to our world, we express gratitude. Gratitude helps us to open further and receive more. Ruiz says that love is the perfect balance between gratitude and generosity.

15

THE PATH OF RELATIONSHIP

Enjoy the sweetness of love without clinging.

—DZOGCHEN PONLOP RINPOCHE

WHEN THE WHOLE BODY is present and humming with life, when the mind is open and the heart shines like the sun, the energy that radiates is love. Practicing opening our hearts and bodies in all the ways we've explored in this book is a physical way to practice love—and clearly love is what the world needs.

It feels so good when we carry an inner smile in our hearts, perhaps even a little smile on our lips, as we bask in the experience of love. Then, inevitably, the complexities of life pour in. Each of us has so many obligations and faces so many junctures in our lives. We bring such a diversity of creative strengths and solutions. We each think, feel, and perceive different things as we share a moment. It is the sharing of difference that creates intimacy. In this way, relationship is diversity, and this diversity inevitably brings conflict. I say, "Up"; you say, "Down." The middle doesn't work for either of us.

It seems illogical. As mammals and pack animals, relationality is fundamental to our beings, yet relationships are so challenging. Illogical—and oh, so real and true. Accepting this dilemma and aspiring to pursue relationship in a healthy and creative manner, perhaps as an intrinsic aspect of one's spiritual life, is "the path of relationship."

Throughout history, the impulse to explore and commit to the spiritual path has led many people to seek withdrawal from relationship in favor of retreat and solitude. Ironically, this impulse often lands them in sanghas, ashrams, and monasteries—places fraught with the complexity of relationship. We can't avoid relationship. Being human mandates that we learn to work with it.

The Dance of Solitude and Connection

One of the great blessings of leaving our ancestral heritage of hunting and gathering is the degree of individual choice that it has afforded us. As hunters and gatherers, leaving the pack generally meant death. For those without power, living within the pack might mean submitting to challenging dictates from those with power.

If you are reading this book, it is because you have the time and freedom to explore your personal spiritual path. This is a privilege and a choice. Even while choosing to explore spirituality as individuals, most of us are also drawn to the companionship, love, and, in some cases, sexuality that come with relating to other humans. How do we do both?

It is undoubtedly difficult to remain true to ourselves and, at the same time, respectful and kind in our relationships—to allow individuality to enhance relationship, and vice versa, in a creative evolution. Can I continue to feel my own body and give my sensations permission to express themselves *while* I am in relationship with others? One important step on this path is to identify your personal style and habits in relating to others. Are you reserved, avoidant, or shy? Do you tend to be open and expansive? Do you think of yourself as needy, clingy, neutral, or mixed? Do you use different strategies in different kinds of relationships? How do you think your relational style affects your relationship with yourself and your spirituality?

Most of us are deeply conditioned to forget our own experience when we relate to others. We lose our mindfulness of body and are only mindful of others. When this happens, we quickly feel overwhelmed and off track in our lives. We push others away. We lose ourselves in relationship. Perhaps we know ways to recover our autonomy through embodiment practices, meditation, or time in nature. At a certain point, we become ready for relationship. We reach out again, perhaps more mindfully this time. Perhaps we can notice the need for solitude before becoming lost. It is a normal and healthy cycle to move in and out of relationship and solitude. We can follow the cycle in more or less healthy ways.

Within the long-term relationships that we maintain through these cycles, the question of fairness often arises: "Are my needs being met by this relationship? If I have a need for connection when you have a need for solitude, shouldn't you give up your solitude at least half the time?" The reality is that the balance does not exist, and relationships are not fundamentally about fairness in the fifty-fifty sense, but rather about negotiation and choice. In this sense, it is of great importance that we be in touch with our own intentions: "What is the purpose of relationship for me in the first place?"

Many years ago, I was present in a small group conversation, and a question about balance in relationship was presented to Dilgo Khyentse Rinpoche. Khyentse Rinpoche was one of my own spiritual teachers and one of the last great Tibetan Buddhist teachers of our time. A mountain of a man who had gone way beyond conventional behavior, he had a smile like John Wayne's and fingernails so long they were distracting. To the student's question about relationship, he replied, "The purpose of relationship is for the spiritual growth of both people."

Interesting. Isn't relationship about survival of the species? Or about getting my needs met? Of course, both of those perspectives are valid and can be seen as true at various moments, yet Rinpoche's perspective shows their partiality. For some of us, the idea of spiritual growth through relationship may also challenge the notion that dedicating one's life to prayer or meditation is the most exalted spiritual path. Maybe that's true for some people, but as those of us in relationships know, no one can bring you to your edge like an intimate partner.

Relationship of any kind can be a tremendous opportunity to see ourselves more clearly and to practice letting go of our egocentric behaviors and perspectives. But that letting go is never complete and final; in the next moment, we have to feel ourselves anew, and then, quite often, it all gets complicated again. When one of my children was tiny and hitting someone or something, I told her to use her words and not her hands. She replied, "But I was jess' 'spressing my feelings." I couldn't help but laugh at this little girl, who had already learned one of the key lessons of Embodiment Practice from her mother and was using it to her advantage. It's such a human process to learn to express our feelings without making a big mess out of everything. From the perspective of Embodiment Practice, yes, express your feelings and let that expression release them. But maturity in this practice means refining our sense of possibility and choice within that expression. With time, we develop the finesse that allows us to express in ways that respond skillfully to our environment without causing harm. To learn how to do this without denying or repressing our feelings and their drive toward expression is a craft we can all practice, with ever-greater skill and creativity, for the rest of our lives.

Explore what is true inside yourself and how that interfaces with others: "Does what I want accord with what you want? Can I be present with myself and share truthfully with you? Can I listen to you and witness your experience, fully and wholeheartedly, *and* stay rooted in my own experience?"

Practicing authenticity in relationship is a natural outgrowth of the maturation of the spiritual path. Building relationships with others is an expression of heart and kindness, an expression of moving out of our isolated sense of self. Out of our own embodiment, we become intimate with ourselves. Out of embodied practices, we open to those around us. This openness is the ground of relational intimacy.

How do we shift out of a mentality in which relationship is supposed to meet our personal needs and desires of the moment? How do we offer ourselves to the path of relationship in the same way we approach the spiritual path? Often when I talk to young people about their relationships, they seemed shocked by the level of difficulty involved and complain that their needs aren't being met. On the other hand, many single people are dissatisfied with living alone. We all have to discern our paths in life. Can we contentedly live alone? If not, can we work with ourselves and our partners to transform conflict into path? This dance between self and other, solitude and contact, is the ever-shifting tide of human life. What does it mean to approach that dance as a spiritual practice?

Mutual Meditation

Sit across from another person. Both of you close your eyes and ground into your own experience. When you feel present and embodied, slowly open your eyes. Notice if seeing the other person pulls you out of your own experience. If so, close your eyes again and reground in yourself; refresh your own embodiment. Eventually, see what happens if you can feel your body and see the other at the same time. Can you arrive at a moment when you are both present in yourselves, with your eyes are open, seeing each other? A miracle!

Embodied Speech

Ground in your own physical presence, and as you're ready, begin slowly reading out loud to yourself. Feel each syllable as you form it. Feel each thought as you articulate it. Relax into thinking and speaking and feeling your body all at the same time.

When you are ready, try talking to yourself in the same way.

If you like, find a partner and practice this same kind of embodied speech in relationship. Make your own embodiment the priority and communicating to the other secondary. This is the only way to reverse our conditioning to ignore ourselves when we are communicating.

Slowly over time, once you have practiced enough,

you will discover that your ability to communicate is actually better when you are grounded in your own embodiment and you maintain a sense of physicality in your speech. You might come to realize that you can only honestly speak from your own experience— "I feel," "I think," "I saw." Once we begin talking about others, we have generally left our own experience.

Circular Attunement

This practice can be done in a group or with just one partner. Begin with individual Embodiment Practice. Feel when your curiosity naturally extends out into your environment and toward those around you.

When that happens, come together with a partner. Invite this person to practice with you, each of you placing your own embodiment as your primary commitment but letting your individual energies extend out into awareness of the other when and as they do.

When you find yourself attending to your partner, remember to continue to feel your own body and keep allowing its energy to move in its own way. Notice when you get swept up with your partner and the relationship and either stop feeling yourself or begin molding yourself into a conceptual relational mode of behavior. This might look like mirroring your partner or behaving in a manner that is complementary to them, but it denies your own experience in some way. At these moments, come back to your own Embodiment Practice, to feeling the sensations in your body right now and letting them move in their own way.

As you practice circular attunement with your partner, you may feel what you are perceiving in your partner and how it affects you internally and mixes with everything you were already feeling, everything that was already moving through you. There are lots of circles moving between each of you in this way, connecting you in attunement. Perhaps you notice that you are receiving energy from the space around you as well.

The Interaction Cycle

In Body-Mind Psychotherapy, we practice a simple form of interacting with others that joins us together in embodiment. This interaction cycle begins with embodiment and then shifts to desire. We witness desire as it moves through the body. I recommend practicing this with yourself first and then trying it with another person.

Begin with your own Embodiment Practice. When you feel grounded in that, ask yourself, "What is it that I want in my life right now? What is emerging? What is this edge of personal development that I am exploring at the moment?"

Once you have a sense of the answer to this, refresh your Embodiment Practice and get back to a fairly neutral place with an easy flow of energy throughout. From this place, think about the desire/edge that you clarified earlier. Be sensitive to whatever shifts this thought evokes in your body.

Once you are clear about what the thought evokes in your body, give those sensations permission to move, breathe, sound, speak, imagine however they like. Let yourself embody your desire/edge as fully as you want to in this moment.

When you feel complete, examine what happened in your Embodiment Practice and how that might support the manifestation of the desire/developmental edge that you articulated.

Practicing the interaction cycle with other people gives us a simple, nonconceptual, noncontrolling, unbiased way to witness and support others when they share with us. Depending on the person's interest in embodiment and intimacy, you may do some of the steps alone or only partially. When people come to you with issues in their lives, first help them to see such issues from a positive, developmental perspective. For example, "If you didn't feel exhausted, what do you imagine you would feel or do differently?" Once they find positive ways to express their desire, encourage them to feel how their bodies respond to the suggestion. For example, you might say, "Close your eyes and think about making more art. Repeat those words over and over: 'I want to make more art. I want to make more art.' Let the idea float around in your body. How does your bodily experience shift?"

When I do this with myself right now, I get lots of shifts. The first is an opening at the top of my heart. As the top of my heart opens, so does my throat. Then the inside of my mouth opens too. The walls of my throat and mouth feel strong and supple. I remember that I have been wanting to sing more.

Meditative Dialogue

As you become grounded in embodied relationship—maintaining presence with another person or people, even while speaking to them—it becomes increasingly possible to engage in "meditative dialogue." During a meditative dialogue, both parties' awareness stays grounded in the core of their bodies. Each practices embodied speech. Every thought that is expressed is given ample time to move all the way through each person's whole being, especially all the way up and down the core of the body.

Each person speaks openly from their own experience, witnessing fully each little shift in experience: "When I heard you say that, I felt some fear, pulling down into my belly. I just thought of my father and how much I miss him."

Give yourselves as much time as you like for your meditative dialogue. When you finish, take some time alone and notice if you perceive anything in solitude that you didn't notice in relationship. Remember this and learn from it.

Finally, the greatest challenge is to maintain awareness during conversations with other people who are not necessarily working with themselves in the same conscious way. So often, we are not open to engaging consciously, noticing how our communications affect others, and sharing how we are affected. In this case—the usual case for most of us in most interactions—

it requires more patience and compassion for ourselves and everyone around us. Nevertheless, it is always possible to invite yourself to remain embodied in your interactions with work colleagues, family, friends, and even strangers.

Embodied Speech in Challenging Conversations

When you are preparing to enter a situation that may offer some challenges, spend a little time doing some Embodiment Practice. Incorporate embodied speech as you do. Work with your speech to span the range from unedited expression—"I'm really mad"—to finding some authentic, heartfelt diplomacy—"That was difficult for me."

As you enter the challenging situation, maintain awareness and allow your body to stay awake and moving a bit. See if all this allows you to meet the challenge more creatively.

Afterward, when you are able do a debriefing Embodiment Practice, even for a couple of minutes, let your body release what it might be holding. Say the words for which you didn't find a diplomatic or satisfying expression. Trust that this will help you continue to grow in embodied maturity.

SACRED SEXUALITY

Several times throughout this book I have noted that we are animals that aspire to the divine. There is no arena in which I find this spectrum of humanity more hilarious than sexuality. One minute we can be gazing tenderly into our lover's eyes, gateways to the divine, and the next minute we are huffing and puffing, as wild as the jungle.

As a behavior mediated by lower brain structures, sexuality is primitive and therefore subject to habit. The intensity of sexual experience is extremely reinforcing. This means every experience—good, bad, and intricately ambivalent—is strongly imprinted on the nervous system and vividly colors each subsequent experience through both perception and behavior. Even our earliest experiences of interacting with others as infants form strong patterns that affect our sexuality. This is a mechanism of habit, and for most people, sexuality is among their most habituated behaviors.

On the other hand, sexuality can be a uniquely creative and potentially healing experience. When we feel safe enough to be vulnerable, we open to new behavior and experiences. This can only occur when there is good communication and cooperation, a lot of caring for ourselves and our partners, and a willingness to pause and shift gears when we lose ourselves or get out of sync with each other, when habit takes over.

As always in embodied spirituality, we begin with cultivating intimacy with ourselves and our bodies over time through our personal embodiment practices. We continue by practicing personal and emotional intimacy with others, learning to feel ourselves while attending to the other. Out of this ground and practice, we enter into sacred sexuality with a commitment to staying present.

Sacred sexuality is a holistic practice. It is not just about arousal and orgasms. Arousal and orgasm are the blossoms of practicing one's own embodiment in loving relationship to another. This necessarily includes lots of circular attunement, some amount of embodied speech and mutual meditation, and lots of naked vulnerability.

If you don't have a partner, you can practice on your own. Stay present as your arousal increases, don't get lost in a habituated pursuit of orgasm.

If your partner isn't interested in discovering sacred sexuality together, you can do your own practice while you are with them. Just keep coming back to the sensations in your body, moment to moment, just like in Embodiment Practice. Slowly, over time, much of this can be communicated indirectly.

I once heard an interview with a bishop or archbishop of the Catholic church. He was advocating that priests be allowed to marry. In essence, he said, "There is so much more spiritual growth that happens in relationship than in celibacy." On the other hand, I once heard Tessa Bielecki, a woman who spent some forty years living in monastic contexts, speak about the ecstatic union with Christ practiced in her order of Carmelite nuns. She had been asked if union with God was just a sublimation of sexuality. She said something like, "Well, yes, from one point of view. However, from our point of view, sex and marriage are a poor substitute for union with God." My heart resonated with the truth of both perspectives.

In Mahayana Buddhism, the vow of the bodhisattva is to support all beings in gaining enlightenment. We are truly in this together. We can only go so far individually, and then our

practice naturally involves others. Within the practice of helping others, we have to continually care for ourselves. Our practice of self-care naturally blossoms into helping others. Perhaps
this is why, as many practitioners age, they no longer feel the
need to make a distinction between their personal path and the
path of relationship.

HUMANITY AND THE UNIVERSE

As our human culture has developed and complexified, as our
numbers have increased, we are living more and more embedded in human nature. We become overwhelmed by humanity—its plight, its sustainability, its demands. At those times,
I like to step back from relationship to other humans and feel
connection to the universe. When you contemplate the role of
humans in the universe, you might notice that it is really only
a thin crust of the surface of the earth and its atmosphere that
has been dominated by human activity. How deep do we have
to go into the earth before we find it undisturbed by human
tampering?

Let go of your breath. Feel the core of your body, from
your pelvic floor to the top of your head. Let go of any
holding that you can contact in your core. Release from
the crown of your head all the way up into the starry
world above your head. Feel the peace and openness of
that world around you and perhaps pouring into you.
Release your pelvis down into the power of the earth's
core. Feel the aliveness and potency of that energy below

you and perhaps rushing into you. Remember that you are a center of this universe. You are a part of the universe. You are the universe.

16

Making Friends with Death

··

DEATH IS THE GREAT mystery of this life, the great adventure of the dedicated spiritual practitioner. Death makes life precious. And it is occurring all the time: every moment, our cells are dying, other creatures are dying. This moment in time ceases. A season passes. A cycle of life is complete. By opening to these cycles of formation and small deaths, we make friends with death itself.

While we are relatively healthy, our bodies have a drive to live and use their complex physiological mechanisms to protect and preserve life. When we are in the process of dying, our physiology shifts to an entirely different mode of operation. Eventually this shift permeates all of our body systems and cells. Experiences such as hunger or dehydration, which are terribly uncomfortable to a body that is busy living, can feel right to a person who is dying. A high level of endorphins can transform discomfort into euphoria. Knowing this can help us relax when we witness the dying process.

LETTING GO PRACTICE

Practicing letting go can help us make friends with death. The first step is to notice when we are clinging.

I once had the opportunity to help a teenage boy hold a chick in his hands. This boy had some neurological and emotional challenges, and he was very excited. I was afraid he would crush the chick. We practiced by having him holding my hand gently, squeezing very lightly. He was able to pick up the chick gently and let his excitement express itself with gentleness rather than force.

We so often hold on to things too tightly. We push. We persist. We use force to get our way. When I notice myself doing this, I say, "Let it go, honey. Let it go." I feel my body and release the forcefulness. I try to hold the preciousness of life gently and with reverence rather than too greedily. When this works, I arrive at a place of peace and gratitude.

Any mindfulness practice can be a practice of letting go. When we are with what is, we let go of what we think should be. We stop holding on. The Serenity Prayer, written by Reinhold Niebuhr in the early 1900s and used widely in the twelve-step movement, is a letting go practice:

> God grant me the serenity to accept the things
>   I cannot change,
> Courage to change the things I can,
> And wisdom to know the difference.

WITNESSING DEATH

In earlier cultures—and some less wealthy countries today—people witnessed death on a daily basis. Without consciously intending to, they accepted death as a normal part of life. In most contemporary cultures, death is almost entirely hidden away. More and more people are terrified of the inevitable. As death becomes removed from daily life in our antiseptic cultures, it is easy to deny that it is coming. We unconsciously develop a strong aversion to death. For this reason, those of us who want to refamiliarize ourselves with death have to practice relaxing into it. One way to do this is to participate in death as it arises in your community. Be available. Seek it out. Offer to visit the dying. Go to the funerals and memorials. Bathe the bodies of your dead friends and family. Practice mindfulness as you do this. Remember to breathe and feel your body.

While someone is dying, and even after they die, sitting with them can be a beautiful experience. At that point, you become the beneficiary. Your loved one can teach you about death and dying, help you learn to relax and be present. If you experience overwhelming emotions, feel them in your body. Grieve, but also look for peace and relaxation during the moments that allow it. Don't make death a bigger deal than it is. Talk kindly to yourself: "Everything is okay." Remember that your loved one is out of pain. Do you still have a sense of their presence? What is the quality that lingers in the death room? How big is that field?

Midwifing Death

Beyond witnessing death, we can help others die. We can talk to them. We can tell them whatever we need to say to let go: "I love you. I forgive you. I know you love me. I know you did your best. You gave me so much. It is okay to go now."

We can stroke their foreheads and give them ice chips during the early phases. We can read to them from inspiring texts. We can say to them, explicitly or implicitly, that it's okay to be dying and they don't need to fight it.

When death comes, whether for ourselves or our loved ones,

we will embody the relationship we have cultivated with death. When we are frightened of death, we resist it. Have you watched someone who is struggling to hold on die anyway? Their faces, their bodies, their breath—all contort in fear and struggle. We can help soothe their fears. We can sing to them or chant or even breathe audibly. Whatever feels right. Midwifing death is truly an embodied practice. We have to feel our way through. The more we have practiced, the less we project our ideas about death onto the one who is dying and the more we are able to listen and perceive what is needed.

My mother-in-law began dying in the hospital, so we brought her to our home. Then she perked right up and proceeded to live, relatively content to spend the next three and a half years lying in bed, talking to her parents and God, waiting for death. We struggled with this, trying physical therapy and proposing the idea of antidepressants. She was appalled. She was not depressed; instead, she described herself as "dying in an exemplary fashion." In fact, that turned out to be true.

Her active dying process took two weeks. Our children were young at the time. During those last two weeks, we spent a lot of time by her bed, loving her, holding her hand, reading a bit, meditating. I taught my children to visualize her spirit as light easing out of her body through the top of her head. The last day, she started a very dramatic version of the death rattle for several hours. It was a rapid, forceful breath, not unlike the yogic breath of fire. Yet during this intense breathing, her eyes remained calm, even loving. She drew our hands to her cheeks. Finally, when she was close to death, I leaned over to my older daughter and said, "Grandma's doing great now. This part is for us." In her full fourteen-year-old wisdom, she pulled herself into a vertical position and said, "Oh, I know!" She proceeded to sit, very still, upright, and present for the next forty-five minutes through her first close experience of death.

My experience of my mother-in-law's actual death was what I can only describe as biblical. I felt her rise serenely out of her body, out of the room, away, away, away. The room seemed filled with golden light and trumpets. After three and a half years of dying practice, nothing seemed to linger. She seemed completely gone.

We left her body undisturbed for three days, as is the Buddhist tradition, to give the mind time to let go of the body. During this time, several of the children's friends asked to see her body. I had them ask their parents for permission, and it seemed to be a wonderful introduction to the peacefulness and normalcy of death. Years later, the same daughter that sat still during her grandmother's last moments was wondering at the struggle people feel with death. At twenty-something, she was able to say, "I've had a good life. If I were to die now, I think I'd be okay with that." I told her I thought that was a gift from her grandmother: "Thanks to Grandma. She gave us all a very positive experience. It changed my relationship to death."

Each death brings its own wisdom. Close to dying, my friend William proclaimed, "Peace, tranquility, and the infinite— that's where I'm going." When his time came, shortly after that statement, he needed only the slightest midwifery—support to lengthen and straighten his spine, a short time of breathing together—and he went on the out-breath.

Arthur, a family friend, beckoned his daughter close to his deathbed and told her, "I'm ready to go, but I don't know how." Wonderfully wise, she said, "Well, Daddy, that's between you and God." He died peacefully just a few hours later.

A student told me about her shamanistic teacher's death. He

gathered his students together for his last drumming circle and said that he would go on the last beat of the drum. And he did!

During the writing of this book, my neighbor's mother had a series of ministrokes and began talking more creatively. When my neighbor Joan went to visit her, she said, "I've got to get out of here. You've got to help me hop." Joan didn't miss a beat: "Momma, I'm here to help you hop."

Preparing for Death Together

I was taught this meditation, created by Thich Nhat Hanh. Stand hand in hand facing your partner. One partner speaks each line and the other partner repeats it.

"I am going to die." . . . "I am going to die."

"You are going to die." . . . "You are going to die."

"All we have is this moment." . . . "All we have is this moment."

If that is too frightening, soften it by saying these phrases first.

"I am here now." . . . "I am here now."

"You are here now." . . . "You are here now."

"All we have is this moment." . . . "All we have is this moment."

PRACTICING DEATH

When you are ready, and if you wish, you can actually practice dying. Do this in whatever manner works for you. Often when I am spent, exhausted from some kind of struggle, I lie down

and let go so completely that the practice of death arises spontaneously. I imagine my body dying, letting go of life, decaying,
dissolving back into the earth. In the right moment, I experience
it as a wonderful relief. Is there a way that you can imagine dying
and practice relaxing with that?

17

WALKING ON WATER: YOUR PATH
OF EMBODIED SPIRITUALITY

Be a lamp unto yourself
Be your own confidence
Hold the truth within yourself
As to the only lamp
—SHAKYAMUNI BUDDHA AT THE TIME
OF HIS DEATH, *MAHAPARANIRVANA SUTRA*

EMBODIED SPIRITUALITY is necessarily very personal. It means different things to all of us and changes as we move through our lives. The commonality is that we pay attention to our lives *as bodies*—reading our beautifully complex senses, organs, and body systems like tea leaves, discerning the path forward based on what is happening now. We move forward with each step, as uncertain as if we were stepping out onto water.

For me, no entryway to this embodied approach to life and spirituality has been more fruitful than the heart. When I first began to inquire more deeply into my heart, I was reluctant to share these inquiries. I feared they would be seen as simplistic, even trite. Slowly over time, I came to appreciate that the simplicity was profound, and the trite was universal. As a child, I had learned to pull my heart back, to keep it hidden for safety. I was deeply committed to that posture in the world. To slowly unpeel all the layers of protection has been a great adventure and a source of deep joy—totally worth all the excruciating pain I had to feel to get there.

My experience with embodied spirituality has shown me that we can move *through* our lives, our bodies, our egos, our habitual emotional patterns—letting them transform, even dissolve, but seeing them as our paths. We don't discard anything. When something touches our hearts, we open to it. The world is new. We take a step into the unknown. In this way each of our spiritual paths unfolds before us uniquely, step by step. A certain amount of faith is required, like walking on water. We have to trust that the next moment will rise up and support us in moving forward.

We are not trying to jump ship to some higher realm. We are trying to let our beings blossom fully. Such a blossoming can organically move us from the small-minded self that has arisen out of our early experiences, our "conditioned self." As we recognize what seems to be an overlay on our innate being, we transform into a truer version of ourselves, the selves we would be if we had not been trained and traumatized out of our beings. This "true self" is our intrinsic physiological way of being, unique to each of us, the unimpeded expression of our genetics and, perhaps, our souls or karmic histories. Moving through our conditioning into our true selves requires perseverance, dedication, and endless patience.

As we start to understand our own conditioning, we can gently rehabilitate ourselves, prune what doesn't work for us, and restructure in ways that allow the best of us to come out. For most of us, working to allow our true selves to blossom evolves through our lifetimes. Understanding this, adults can support young people by seeking to discern their unique qualities, witnessing their true selves. Through this witnessing, we all learn more about expressing ourselves in the world, how to get along with others in our own particular way.

For some of us, in this lifelong process of excavating the true self, we might also begin to stumble into an open space, what in some traditions is called "true nature." True nature extends beyond the true self. Just as, in embodied spirituality, we do not transcend the self but rather allow the true self to evolve out of its conditioning, so we can allow the true self to open further into true nature however it chooses to do so. True nature is unbounded awareness. It is a natural expression of our true selves that is not fixated on the self. As we open to true nature, even for a moment, it catalyzes the process of deconstructing the conditioned self and allowing the true self to emerge more easily. True nature is an organic experience of the true self as it naturally evolves into openness. It is there within us. All we have to do is get out of the way.

SPIRITUAL MATERIALISM

On the other hand, when we push ourselves toward such an experience, it hardens. It congeals. It becomes a conceptual facade, a caricature of itself. This is what Chögyam Trungpa Rinpoche called *spiritual materialism*, an attempt to acquire something that is beyond acquisition, something that is born, instead, from relinquishing, from letting go. The mind that wants to become enlightened never will. Most people on a spiritual path have moments of spiritual materialism arise frequently. When we notice thoughts of ambition or acquisition, we can let go of them. We can feel our bodies soften and open as we return to humility and exploration. We let go again and again. And again, and again.

Spiritual Bypass

When we hide from our very real emotions and life challenges in a pseudo spirituality, this is a *spiritual bypass*. We avoid reality and cling to a fantasy. We don't see ourselves clearly, but develop a persona, a facade. We become a caricature of ourselves in the name of spirituality. If we persist with this strategy, it can solidify into spiritual materialism. Again, when we notice these inevitable attempts to avoid pain and uncertainty, we come back to now. Feel our bodies. Soften into this reality. Accept what is and continue from there.

Cycles

These cycles continually arise. Without realizing it, we slip back into trying to be something or someone, to be better, to be good. This kind of ego activity quickly becomes burdensome and rigid. We notice it. We let go. Often this letting go is uncomfortable, but we can learn to relax with it. We can come back to the moment and back to our bodies. The ego activity inevitably takes on some kind of postural effort. Our heads push forward. Our hearts hide and pull back. Our chest or belly collapses. Whatever. When we notice how we have distorted ourselves, we can return to the simplicity of a neutral alignment. In this neutrality, we feel free. And then the next cycle begins, moments of freedom and liberation follow moments of ego crystalizing, which can be followed by moments of letting go—small deaths. In these small deaths, we let go of a form that we created and inhabited. There is open space.

Meditation on Relaxing into True Nature

Take a moment to feel your body and the space around you. Contemplate the idea of your true self. Imagine that bits of your conditioned self can release each time you exhale. Release as much as you like this way. Give yourself time to let any emotional or physical intensity unwind and release, if possible. See if it feels safe to rest into all of what is happening inside you—your true self. Whatever is arising, open to it. If you are comfortable within yourself and this moment, then rest as deeply into it as you are able. Let go into it. Let go further . . . and further. Then do it again . . . and again. Relax all the while. No effort.

If you go far enough, perhaps you will glimpse the reality that this thing you call your "self" is really just awareness that doesn't belong to you or anything else. This is true nature. As you experience this, let it rest effortlessly in whatever space arises.

As a young practitioner, I tried to keep my embodiment practices separate from my meditation practices. I felt that this was a form of respect for both traditions, traditions that seemed to have little connection. But as both practices developed, their innate unity revealed itself to me.

Sensing fluidity was the first of my embodiment practices that overflowed the banks of the artificial boundaries I had created. As I practiced fluidity more and more fully in my life, it established itself as a basic way of living. After a number of years, I didn't have to remind myself about fluidity anymore. It took over as my default operating mode. In fact, our natural organismic functioning is innately fluid, based on the evolution of life within seawater. Fluidity is the ultimate mode of life, so when we stop obstructing it, it naturally reasserts itself.

Without intentionally choosing it, fluidity crept into my meditation practice more and more over the years. There was no way to control it, and in any case, I could think of no reason that I should. Despite my initial caution about mixing traditions, I came to recognize that meditation practice is aimed toward helping us become more fluid.

Whenever I felt overwhelmed or out of sync in life and meditation, I would remember fluidity and use it as a support to get through whatever challenges I was facing. After a number of years of integrating fluidity on deeper and deeper levels, cellular consciousness emerged as a link to an even greater level of aliveness and creativity than I had found within the world of fluidity. If I felt stuck or weary, I would remember my cells and they would spark into aliveness. With this awareness, I stepped out of the known world into a world of infinite possibility and energy. This was my creative edge for a number of years.

Then I started to recognize the experience of pulsation and the possibility of totally immersing myself in that world. It felt very similar to scuba diving—that whole different reality existing right on the other side of the familiar world. As I was able to rest more and more deeply in the pulsation of my heart, I began to feel all of the other pulsatory rhythms wrapping around it— layers and layers of pulsation, nesting together in a polyrhythmic world. Entering this pulsatory world was a gentle shedding of anxiety and separateness. It was a gateway into the unitive state that allows life to unfold effortlessly without my needing to intend or direct. So, the practices of fluidity, cellular consciousness, and heart pulsation were my primary entry points into the unitive state. As I went deeper into pulsatory awareness, all those entry points came together.

Who knows what will emerge next for me? Who knows how *your* path of embodied spirituality will unfold? I don't know, you don't know, and there's no need to know. I am reminded of the Zen koan, "Not knowing is nearest." The not knowing, in this sense, doesn't mean zoning out. It means moving forward in your life with less attachment to what has come before, finding your way more through practice than through habit.

Six Principles of Embodied Spirituality

As you've seen in this book, I recommend Embodiment Practice as an approach to embodied spirituality. I have found that most people experience their spirituality opening up and enlivening when they allow more exploration and movement into their meditative or contemplative practices. But whether you choose to focus on formal Embodiment Practice as I teach it or another of the many kinds of embodiment practice—meditation, yoga, tai chi, a somatic discipline, mindful sitting and walking, or something else—I think you will find your practice enriched by continually returning to the conjunction of embodiment and spirituality.

In the process of exploring embodied spirituality, I have found these principles to be inherent across different experiences. I offer them here for your contemplation:

⚕ Spiritual states, and our drive to realize them, are innate—our human birthright.

⚕ Only we can discern the unique direction and potential of our personal path.

⚕ The natural wisdom of our bodies and our lives emerges as path if we listen to and allow our sensations to express themselves in the moment.

⚕ The wisdom of nature is constantly available to us, and it is *our* nature to live in connection with all life—beings, the planet itself, the elements, the sun, the moon, and the stars.

⚕ Human development is possible throughout our life spans. Cultivating aliveness and flow in our bodies potentiates our development on all levels, including spiritually if we allow it. This is our path.

⚕ Relationality and emotionality, as they naturally arise, are integral aspects of an embodied spiritual path and cannot be denied or put aside without stopping our developmental flow.

Continuing Our Growth

All the various practices I have introduced in this book, no matter their different means and emphases, have the same goal: to help us feel what is emerging in the moment, to support our natural and unique growth and development. Engaging with ourselves in this way is heartening and inspiring. We feel ourselves more, and we feel more ourselves. We have experiences of truth, freedom, and peace. We also encounter challenges. We dig deeper into the conundrum of our personalities. These are part of the package. We feel more of the good, and we feel the problems more acutely.

How do we support ourselves and each other to ride these challenging times without giving up? Keep an embodied perspective and marry it to a spiritual perspective. Remember what a strange thing it is to be human, not an easy path at all. Finally, appreciate that we humans have a strange and wonderful mandate as part of this world, to make our way through the many dark nights of the soul that are inevitable parts of each human path and still marvel at the process.

The four foundations of mindfulness can offer a framework for tracking your spiritual development.

FOUR FOUNDATIONS OF MINDFULNESS	
1.	Mindfulness of body
2.	Mindfulness of feeling
3.	Mindfulness of mind
4.	Mindfulness of phenomena

Is your awareness of each of these four aspects of life growing? Is it broadening? Deepening? Sustaining through more of your life? Ultimately, you can aspire to be present throughout each moment of existence.

The Four Foundations of Mindfulness Meet the Four Steps of Embodied Spirituality

Pause for a moment and become mindful of what is happening in and around you right now. The first step of embodied spirituality: open your heart. Feel your heart area, reflect on how your relationship to opening your heart has grown during the reading of this book. Feel your breath. Let your heart open.

The first foundation of mindfulness is mindfulness of body. That is also the second step of embodied spirituality: feel your body. Notice whatever is happening in your body right now. Notice the details and the overall flow of energy. Sit with this as long as you choose.

Perhaps at this point, some sense of your emotional tone and feeling states has emerged already. Notice that. The second foundation of mindfulness is mindfulness of feeling. Are full-fledged emotions happening within you right now? If so, give them room to emerge as fully as they want. If not, notice the subtle emotional tones that exist in every moment and every sensation. Whatever you discover, *allow* all of these feelings, sensations, and energetic flows to reveal themselves more fully. That is the third step of embodied spirituality: allowing. Once you get good at the first two foundations of mindfulness—body and feeling—they tend to come together. In order to develop fully, they require permission. Allow all that you sense and feel to spread out, unwind, breathe, and open.

Next, notice what is happening in your mind right now. Is it resting? Is there a lot of thinking? Is there a mental engagement that feels habitual? Let all of your internal mindfulness exist together, spread out, and overlap.

Finally, sense the space around you. Feel your internal mindfulness connect to the external world. Give this awareness permission to grow, to spread out, to move as far out into space as it can go and still stay connected to your core flow. Feel the continuity between the internal and the external. This is connection. This is the unitive state. This fourth step of embodied spirituality, connecting, happens naturally in the wake of each of the four foundations of mindfulness if you allow it. In this way, they all weave together.

Our bodies form our histories, our habitual patterns, karma in the flesh. Emotions, interactions, and actions layer in our tissues like geologic levels of earth. However, this is not fixed. As we open our hearts and allow our bodies to wake up to their own aliveness, these layers can be felt and released. Our bodies can regain their innate state of ease, lightness, and connection.

Thank you for the openness and perseverance it takes to get through a book like this. Pausing to feel, practice, and reflect is not the way most of us have been taught to read. And truly, for these practices to take hold in your being and become your own, you might have to go back through the book repeatedly over a period of time. Whatever the case, I hope your personal approach to embodied spirituality continues to blossom and grow for the rest of your life.

May you continue to find your way.
May your embodied spirituality mature and ripen
to its fullest capacity.
May all beings find their own way and develop
to their fullest capacity.

Epilogue: Teachings from a Star

....

THROUGH THE SMALL crack between my curtains, a bright blue star shines so brightly it wakes me from a deep sleep. I look at it for a few moments and fall back to sleep.

Later, in the light of day, I remember the star, and it is so large, so bright in my imagination—it seems to pulsate. Each time of remembering, it has a powerful effect—my head floats upward, lengthening my spine, my consciousness feels . . . suspended. I am floating in space . . . as if awareness itself is suspended by its own brightness, floating effortlessly in vast space.

And then, I remember something Chögyam Trungpa Rinpoche said, something I contemplated for a long time. He said, "I want you to float, so to speak, and become real by floating."

When I remember the star, my mind expands out into space. There is a timeless moment and sense of unity without boundaries. Is this what Trungpa Rinpoche meant by "becoming real"?

As a young person, I never dreamed of arriving at this moment in my life, this feeling of fullness and connection to myself, my body, and my world. This fullness has given me the courage to write about embodied spirituality. As a young person, I was quiet and diligent. I didn't understand my path in life. I didn't have words for my own internal states. It took a tremendous amount of processing, often in difficulty and grief, to even begin to shed this huge burden of my confusion. Though the details of each of our lives are different, we all struggle to wake up to who we are. As this process of waking up continues, I am struck by the amount of perseverance that is required of me and of all of us.

Nature was and continues to be the ground. Studying the body has been the hidden treasure, the wish-fulfilling mirror. Studying psychology and practicing communication make up the grindstone that sharpens my understanding of the nuances of human relationships. Practicing mindfulness is the gateway.

Recently, I took five days at home for a meditation retreat. I have done years of retreat in my life, but this one was different. I listened more deeply to my body and its path. To do this, I felt the sensations in my body, but I also listened below the sensations, or perhaps *through* them, to a sense of what was trying to unfold within me. I trusted myself more, rested when I needed to rest, adapted practices more and more personally to the moment. This resulted in a much more powerful retreat than I had ever experienced.

My heart felt open to this huge world around me. There was so much light inside me and around me. I felt my life as a spark within the brilliance of the universe. I felt a part of it all, at one with it all, free of the oppressive concerns about myself and my place in the world. All my petty concerns dropped away. No more questioning if I was doing enough or doing it right. It sounds so trite as I write it, but it felt miraculous. I never thought I would experience such a thing. All my decades of meditating and studying spirituality, doing the weird alchemy of connecting the body to the psyche and spirituality, and suddenly this experience was simply present. It was available to me whenever I tuned in, and I stayed tuned in for most of the five days.

Since the retreat, as I have returned to my work, I feel very naked. So many of my familiar protective defenses are gone. I am faced with the intensity of integrating a new level of openness. I don't want to don my familiar armor again, but to avoid this, I have to go slow, sift each experience carefully and consciously through my body and mind until I find an understanding deep enough to be at peace with the reality I am facing.

Always, I am feeling my body. I am noticing mental beliefs, attitudes, positions that are stopping life from flowing through my body. I am seeking to release those and see what happens. I am asking myself if I can trust what is happening inside me and around me. By trusting, I can allow myself to be nakedly present within it and then see what happens next.

I hope this book has helped you find or continue your own path of embodied spirituality.

Acknowledgments

MY FIRST SPIRITUAL TEACHER, Cornelia Fla-
nary Henderson, a child of Appalachia and a devout
Christian, taught me to be a good person, to tell the truth, to
help others, and to pray each day for those most in need. Though
she has been gone for over a decade, I still feel her steady hand
keeping me grounded and honest.

Tibetan Buddhism has provided me with a deep understanding of the science of the mind, and its wonderfully structured
meditation curriculum has guided me through my entire adult
life. Though I have benefited greatly from its teachings and
teachers, I have always had a mistrust of organized religion.
Tibetan Buddhism comes from a very patriarchal, medieval
culture, and it is undergoing tremendous change right now. It
continues to give me so much, but only as I am willing to break
through oppression inwardly and outwardly. I have had two
close Tibetan Buddhist teachers in my life. The first was Chögyam Trungpa Rinpoche. If not for his outrageously direct and
personal style, I doubt I would ever have dedicated my life to
spiritual development. Thankfully, Dzogchen Ponlop Rinpoche
has made it so much easier and politically palatable to continue
on that path. Even more important, he has helped me to under-

stand and contextualize my own experience within the very codified Tibetan Buddhist context.

I first met Bonnie Bainbridge Cohen, my Body-Mind Centering® teacher, in 1979. As I wrote in the foreword to her first book, *Sensing, Feeling, and Action*, "She captured me with a single remark. I asked her, 'What are all these blockages in the body? Where do they come from?' She said, 'It's mind watching itself.' This answer was the most direct and enigmatic I could imagine, and its meaning has continued to unfold for me over the years." As I pursued Tibetan Buddhism, I became increasingly sensitive to its male domination. I longed for a female spiritual teacher. It took me several decades to realize that I had had one all along.

In addition to the many profound people who have explicitly been my teachers, I have learned and grown in essential ways from each and every person in my life: family of all generations, friends, colleagues, students, and clients. Thank you, thank you, thank you.

This book has benefited greatly from its early readers and advisors: Mary Sweet, Meredith Fuller, Pat Ogden, Jane Ellison, Kimberly Gladysz, and Christian Dillo. In addition, to her early reading, Mary Sweet has labored with love over the intricate details of every drawing. Anatomical drawings offer myriad aesthetic and technical challenges. Mary has met them all with alacrity and creativity. Finally, I have been blessed with editors who truly understand what I am trying to communicate here. I cannot even imagine how lucky I am to have stumbled into such rare combinations of body awareness and literary prowess—the greatest of thanks to Matt Zepelin and Eli Gottlieb, without either of whom this particular book would truly not exist.

NOTES

1. For more on this topic, see S. Paddison, *The Hidden Power of the Heart: Achieving Balance and Fulfillment in a Stressful World* (Boulder Creek, CA: HeartMath, 1992).
2. William James, "What Is an Emotion?" in *Collected Essays and Reviews*, ed. Ralph Barton Perry (New York: Longmans, Green, 1920), 248.
3. From the "Neiye" chapter in *Guanzi*, quoted in Elisabeth Rochat and Claude Larre, *The Heart: In Ling Shu Chapter 8* (Taos, NM: Redwing Books, 1991), 83.
4. Unless citing published material, all references to specific people are disguised, amalgamated, or otherwise altered so as to protect the privacy of the individuals.
5. For more on this topic, see Jaak Panksapp, *The Archaeology of Mind: Neuroevolutionary Origins of Human Emotions* (New York: W.W. Norton, 2012).
6. Thomas Hora, *Dialogues in Metapsychiatry* (Orange, CA: PAGL Press, 1986), 64.
7. Eric Lee, "From the Heart of the World: The Elder Brothers' Warning," May 21, 2016. www.sustainable.soltechdesigns.com/elder-brothers-warning.html. To read more about the Kogi and their efforts to preserve their traditional homelands, visit www.koginkasewalunafoundation.org/home or www.taironatrust.org.
8. For more on the five fundamental actions, see Susan Aposhyan, *Natural Intelligence: Body-Mind Integration and Human Development* (Baltimore, MD: Williams and Wilkins, 1999).
9. Daniel Goleman and Richard J. Davidson, *Altered Traits: Science Reveals How Meditation Changes Your Mind, Brain, and Body* (New York: Avery, 2017).
10. Sonjan, "The Majesty Field" (unpublished manuscript, 2020).

11. Bruce Lipton, *The Biology of Belief* (Santa Rosa, CA: Mountain of Love/ Elite Books, 2005), 146.

12. This is a different number than I have used in the past. It is based on the most recent scientific estimation in Eva Bianchoni, Allison Piovesan, Federica Facchin, et al., "An Estimation of the Number of Cells in the Human Body," *Annals of Human Biology* 40, no. 6 (2013): 463–71.

13. Quoted in Aposhyan, *Natural Intelligence*, 149.

14. To read about Lacks's life and the history of her cells, including the ethical issues surrounding their use for research, see Rebecca Skloot, *The Immortal Life of Henrietta Lacks* (New York: Broadway Books, 2011).

15. Bonnie Bainbridge Cohen, *Sensing, Feeling, and Action* (Northampton, MA: Contact Editions, 2008), 157.

16. Don Miguel Ruiz and Janet Mills, *The Four Agreements* (San Rafael, CA: Amber-Allen Publishing, 1997).

17. Brian Swimme and Thomas Berry, *The Universe Story* (New York: HarperCollins Publishers, 1992).

18. Allan Schore, *Affect Regulation and the Origin of the Self* (New York: Routledge, 2016), 75.

BIBLIOGRAPHY

Aposhyan, Susan. *Natural Intelligence: Body-Mind Integration and Human Development*. Baltimore, MD: Williams and Wilkins, 1999.

——. "An Attitude of Prayerfulness." *Currents* 17, no. 1 (2017): 62–65.

——. *Body-Mind Psychotherapy: Principles, Techniques, and Practical Applications*. New York: W. W. Norton, 2004.

Bainbridge Cohen, Bonnie. *Sensing, Feeling, and Action*. Northampton, MA: Contact Editions, 2008.

Bianchoni, Eva, Allison Piovesan, Federica Facchin, et al. "An Estimation of the Number of Cells in the Human Body." *Annals of Human Biology* 40, no. 6 (2013): 463–71.

Gendlin, Eugene. *Focusing*. New York: Bantam, 1981.

Goldberg, Natalie. *Writing Down the Bones*. Boulder, CO: Shambhala Publications, 1986.

Goleman, Daniel, and Richard J. Davidson *Altered Traits: Science Reveals How Meditation Changes Your Mind, Brain, and Body*. New York: Avery, 2017.

Harvey, William. *On the Motion of the Heart and Blood in Animals*. Buffalo, NY: Prometheus, 1993.

Hora, Thomas. *Dialogues in Metapsychiatry*. Orange, CA: PAGL Press, 1986.

Lee, Eric. "From the Heart of the World: The Elder Brothers' Warning." May 21, 2016. www.sustainable.soltechdesigns.com/elder-brothers-warning.html.

Lipton, Bruce. *The Biology of Belief*. Santa Rosa, CA: Mountain of Love/Elite Books, 2005.

Lowen, Alexander. *The Spirituality of the Body*. Hinesburg, VT: The Alexander Lowen Foundation, 1990.

Lowrey, Jim. *Taming Untameable Beings*. Redondo Beach, CA: Blue Horse, 2015.

Machado, Antonio. *There Is No Road.* Buffalo, NY: White Pine Press, 2003.

Margulis, Lynn, and Dorian Sagan. *Microcosmos: Four Billion Years of Microbial Evolution.* Berkeley: University of California Press, 1986.

Mukpo, Mipham J. *Turning the Mind Into an Ally.* New York: Penguin Books, 2003.

Paddison, S. *The Hidden Power of the Heart: Achieving Balance and Fulfillment in a Stressful World.* Boulder Creek, CA: HeartMath, 1992.

Panksapp, Jaak. *The Archaeology of Mind: Neuroevolutionary Origins of Human Emotions.* New York: W.W. Norton. 2012.

Pearsall, Paul. *The Heart's Code.* New York: Broadway, 1998.

Rochat, Elisabeth, and Claude Larre. *The Heart: In Ling Shu Chapter 8.* Cambridge, UK: Monkey Press, 1991.

Ruiz, don Miguel, *The Four Agreements.* San Rafael, CA: Amber-Allen Publishing, 1997.

Rumi, Jalal al-Din. *The Essential Rumi.* Translated by C. Barks and J. Moyne. San Francisco: Harper, 2004.

Satprem. *The Mind of the Cells.* New York: Institute for Evolutionary Research, 1982.

Schore, Allan. *Affect Regulation and the Origin of the Self.* Hillsdale, NJ: Erlbaum, 1994.

Sonjan. "The Majesty Field." Unpublished manuscript, 2020.

Swimme, Brian, and Thomas Berry. *The Universe Story.* New York: HarperCollins Publishers, 1992.

Trungpa, Chögyam. *Cutting Through Spiritual Materialism.* Boulder, CO: Shambhala Publications, 2007.

———. *Evam.* DVD. Canada: Kalapa Recordings, 2009.

———. *Shambhala: The Sacred Path of the Warrior.* Boston: Shambhala Press, 2007.

Welwood, John. *Toward a Psychology of Awakening.* Boston: Shambhala Publications, 2000.